Workbook
LOW BEGINNING

OXFORD
PICTURE
DICTIONARY

THIRD EDITION

Jane Spigarelli

OXFORD
UNIVERSITY PRESS

198 Madison Avenue
New York, NY 10016 USA

Great Clarendon Street, Oxford, ox2 6DP, United Kingdom

Oxford University Press is a department of the University of Oxford.
It furthers the University's objective of excellence in research, scholarship,
and education by publishing worldwide. Oxford is a registered trade
mark of Oxford University Press in the UK and in certain other countries

ISBN: 978-0-19-4511247

Printed in China

This book is printed on paper from certified and well-managed sources

ACKNOWLEDGEMENTS

Illustrations by: Argosy Publishing: 71, 92, 96 (top), 98 (top), 100 (top), 115
(pills, cream, tablets, cough medicine, inhaler), 206; Lori Anzalone: 13 (map);
Barbara Bastian: 214; Ken Batelman: 159, 229 (top); Fanny Mellet Berry: 123,
183; Arlene Boehm: 51; Kevin Brown: 37, 54, 68, 91(bottom), 102, 152, 189;
Seb Carmagajevac/Beehive Illustration: 23, 44, 136; Andrea Champlin: 55
(bottom), 248; Mike DiGiorgio: 67 (lower left), 69, 75, 78; Nic DiLauro/Contact
Jupiter: 5, 25, 47 (top), 250, 254; Mike Gardner: 7 (top), 33 (top), 39 (top), 49 (top),
71, 97, 114, 134, 182, 177, 233, 236; Garth Glazer/AA Reps: 106; Glenn Gustafson:
11 (top), 14, 77, 94, 119 (bottom), 138 (top), 179, 190, 201 (top); Ben Hasler: 56, 59,
197, 93, 225, 256; Betsy Hayes: 137 (bottom); Janos Jantner/Beehive Illustration:
17, 29, 41, 45, 60, 89, 103, 106, 111, 124, 151, 172, 200; Mike Kasun/Munro
Campagna: 224; John Kurtz: 112, 121, 141, 167, 178; Debbie Lofaso: 4, 48, 110,
113; Denis Luzuriaga: 34, 40, 85, 101, 110 (top), 122, 176, 203 (bottom), 247;
Chris Lyons/Lindgren & Smith: 203 (top); Scott MacNeill: 18, 66, 70, 79 (top), 86,
87 (chart); Alan Male/Artworks Illustration: 216; Paul Mirocha/The Wiley Group:
222; Marc Mones/AA Reps: 34, 231, 251; Laurie O'Keefe: 107; Chris Pavely: 73 (top),
82, 105 (top), 117 (top), 137 (top), 139, 148, 244, 259; Jon Rogers/AA Reps: 142, 188,
199, 241, 249, 258; Robert Roper/Wilkinson Studios: 2, 8, 32, 58, 65, 83 (top), 87
(top), 104, 120, 138 (bottom), 221; Zina Saunders: 10, 28, 36, 38, 76, 84, 96 (bottom),
99; Marco Schaaf/AA Reps: 61, 132, 153, 196, 198, 234 (top); Robert Schoolcraft/
Artworks Illustration: 117 (top), 123 (top); Rob Schuster: 13 (chart), 14, 21 (top),
37, 48, 63, 67 (top), 74, 79, 116, 133, 149, 150 (right), 162, 186, 207, 219, 232, 243;
Ben Shannon: 3 (top), 22, 42, 62, 81(top), 91 (top), 98 (bottom), 108, 118, 131 (top),
146, 147, 165, 169, 180, 181, 192, 227, 242, 245, 257; Dan Sharp/The Neis Group: 3
(bottom), 6, 24, 43, 50, 80, 90 (bottom), 95 (top), 129 (top), 161, 173, 185, 193, 228,
239 (top), 252; Pete Smith/Beehive Illustration: 64, 72, 88, 100 (bottom), 135, 141,
195, 226, 246; Sam Tomasello: 211 (top); Samuel Velasco (5W Infographics) 210,
211, 212, 213; Ralph Voltz/Deborah Ltd.: 12, 35, 57, 130, 145, 158, 255; Laura
Wills: 143, 174; Philip Williams/Deborah Wolfe Ltd.: 46, 53, 125, 128, 157, 187,
230; Craig Zuckerman: 113 (top).

Chapter icons: Anna Sereda

Pronk&Associates: 7 (graph), 9, 20, 21 (chart), 27, 31, 33 (chart), 39 (list), 47 (graph),
49 (crossword), 63 (pie chart), 67 (shopping list), 73 (guide), 79 (graph), 81 (check),
83 (ads), 90 (chart), 95 (receipt), 105 (chart), 109 (crossword), 111, 115 (ad), 129
(schedule), 131 (chart), 150 (list), 156, 160 (pie chart), 183 (pay stub), 171 (graph),
168, 175, 179 (crossword), 194, 201 (pie chart), 205, 208, 215, 217 (article), 229
(brochure), 235, 237 (crossword), 239 (graph), 240.

*The publishers would like to thank the following for their kind permission to reproduce
photographs:* p.10 Andrey_Popov/Shutterstock; p. 15 Daniel M Ernst/Shutterstock;
p. 26 Fat Jackey/Shutterstock, mattesimages/Shutterstock, Fat Jackey/Shutterstock,
Sascha Burkard/Shutterstock, Dennis Kitchen Studio Inc./OUP, nimon/Shutterstock,
[I]n Vdovin / Alamy Stock Photo, Ivan Vdovin / Alamy Stock Photo, Ivan Vdovin /
[Alam]y Stock Photo; p. 30 Milica Nistoran/Shutterstock, thechatat/Shutterstock,
[...]re/Shutterstock, Flickr/OUP, wavebreakmedia/Shutterstock, ZouZou/

Shutterstock; p. 43 Wavebreak Media ltd / Alamy Stock Photo; p.48 tiketta
Sangasaeng/Shutterstock, Susan Law Cain/Shutterstock; p. 52 Mark William
Richardson/Shutterstock, Fun Fun Photo/Shutterstock, romakoma/Shutterstock,
Kenneth Sponsler/Shutterstock, rawmn/Shutterstock, Cultura Creative (RF) /
Alamy; p. 55 Anita Patterson Peppers/Shutterstock, Stock Up/ Shutterstock, AS
Food studio/Shutterstock, M. Unal Ozmen/Shutterstock, Evgeny Karandaev/
Shutterstock, horiyan/Shutterstock; p. 78 Ekaterina Kondratova/Shutterstock,
VICHAILAO/Shutterstock, Ekaterina Kondratova/Shutterstock, Sergey Lapin/
Shutterstock, Prisma/ SuperStock, vvoe/Shutterstock; p. 94 Fruit Cocktail Creative/
Shutterstock, Ruslan Semichev/Shutterstock, Shutterstock/OUP; p. 95 Dmitry
Kalinovsky/Shutterstock; p. 96 Tarzhanova/Shutterstock, Tarzhanova/Shutterstock,
ConstantinosZ/Shutterstock, Everything/Shutterstock; p. 109 John Gollop / Alamy,
Lipskiy/Shutterstock, Mediablitzimages / Alamy, Art65395/Shutterstock,
Nik Merkulov/Shutterstock; p.113 cyano66/iStockphoto; p. 138 AVAVA/Shutterstock,
p. 140 Orhan Cam/Shutterstock, Horizon International Images Limited / Alamy;
p. 154 TSpider/Shutterstock, Thomas Schneider/imag / imageBROKER /SuperStock,
Bruno Ferrari/Shutterstock, DreamPictures/Shannon Faulk / SuperStock, waku/
Shutterstock, Thor Jorgen Udvang/Shutterstock; p. 163 Susan Chiang/Getty Images;
p. 166 Marilyn Nieves/Getty Images, BOONROONG/Shutterstock, moodboard / Alamy
Stock Photo, ArCaLu/Shutterstock, Alexey Stiop/Shutterstock, Arjuna Kodisinghe/
Shutterstock, tusharkoley/Shutterstock, Chris Pancewicz / Alamy Stock Photo,
Phil Boorman/Getty Images; p. 170 Robert Kneschke/Shutterstock, Tyler Olson/
Shutterstock, wavebreakmedia/Shutterstock, Hero Images/Getty Images, Juice
Images/ SuperStock, Minerva Studio/Shutterstock; p. 171 Sergiy Zavgorodny/
Shutterstock, michaeljung/Shutterstock, Claudia Wiens / Alamy, Flashon Studio/
Shutterstock, RubberBall / RubberBall; p. 184 Visionsi/Shutterstock, Cultura Creative
(RF) / Alamy, Arsenik/Getty Images, Ian Allenden / Alamy, Tony Tremblay/Getty
Images, Jon Feingersh/Getty Images; p. 186 Gerald Bernard/Shutterstock, Ingram/
OUP, chuyuss/Shutterstock, George Doyle/Getty Images, Mitja Mladkovic / Alamy;
p. 191 Denis Dryashkin/Shutterstock, Blazej Lyjak/Shutterstock, Aleksandr Bryliaev/
Shutterstock, Jiw Ingka/Shutterstock, Design Collection/Shutterstock; p. 209 Culver
Pictures, Inc. /SuperStock, Grant Terry/Shutterstock, Glasshouse Images / Alamy,
Classic Vision / age fotostock/SuperStock; p. 213 vgstudio/Shutterstock; p. 214
dotshock/Shutterstock, Ursula Perreten/Shutterstock, rickyd/Shutterstock; p. 220
Nyvlt-art/Shutterstock, Gallinago_media/Shutterstock, Jessmine/Shutterstock,
BOONCHUAY PROMJIAM/Shutterstock, Butterfly Hunter/Shuttesrstock, Aksenova
Natalya/Shutterstock; p.223 Stephanie Dalen/Shutterstock, Volodymyr Burdiak/
Shutterstock, Francois van Heerden/Shutterstock, Wolfgang Zwanzger/Shutterstock;
p. 234 Miguel Pereira/Getty images, PCN Photography / Alamy, Blue Jean Images
/ Blue SuperStock, Manuel Sulzer / Cultura Limited/SuperStock, Jeff Gross/Getty
Images, Arthur Tilley/Getty Images; p. 237 Michael Dechev/Shutterstock, Bombaert
Patrick / Alamy, yuyangc/Shutterstock, Maks Narodenko/Shutterstock, Tatiana
Popova/Shutterstock, Mtsaride/Shutterstock; p. 240 Valentin Valkov/Shutterstock,
photosync/Shutterstock, gmstockstudio/Shutterstock, Olga Popova/Shutterstock,
Titania/Shutterstock, HSNphotography/Shutterstock; p. 244 Vereshchagin Dmitry/
Shutterstock, OUP Picturebank, Photodisc/OUP, cowardlion/Shutterstock, Photodisc/
OUP, lem/Shutterstock; p. 253 Minerva Studio/Shutterstock, IMAGEMORE Co,
Ltd./Getty Images, BSIP/UIG/Getty Images, Andrey_Popov/Shutterstock, Tatiana
Popova/Shutterstock, Vlad Teodor/Shutterstock, naka-stockphoto/Shutterstock,
Shutterstock/OUP, Somos/OUP, Uppercut/OUP.

*The publisher would like to thank the following for their permission to
reproduce copyrighted material:*
127, 136–137: USPS Corporate Signature, Priority Mail, Express Mail, Media Mail,
Certified Mail, Ready Post, Airmail, Parcel Post, Letter Carrier Uniform, Postal Clerk
Uniform, Flag and Statue of Liberty, Postmark, Post Office Box, Automated Postal
Center, Parcel Drop Box, Round Top Collection Mailbox are trademarks of the United
States Postal Service and are used with permission.

Welcome to the Oxford Picture Dictionary Third Edition Workbooks

The *Low Beginning, High Beginning,* and *Low Intermediate Workbooks* that accompany *The Oxford Picture Dictionary* have been designed to provide meaningful and enjoyable practice of the vocabulary that students are learning. These workbooks supply high-interest contexts and real information for enrichment and self-expression.

The Oxford Picture Dictionary Third Edition provides unparalleled support for vocabulary teaching and language development.

• New and expanded topics including job search, career planning, and digital literacy prepare students to meet the requirements of their daily lives.

• Updated activities prepare students for work, academic study, and citizenship.

• Oxford 3000 vocabulary ensures students learn the most useful and important words.

Page-for-page correlation with the Dictionary

The *Workbook* pages conveniently correspond to the pages of the *Picture Dictionary*. For example, if you are working on page 50 in the *Dictionary*, the activities for this topic, Apartments, will be found on page 50 in all three *Picture Dictionary Workbooks*.

Consistent easy-to-use format

All topics in the *Low Beginning Workbook* follow the same easy-to-use format. Exercise 1 introduces students to the target words in the Word List and provides a task designed to review meaning. The tasks in Exercise 1 offer learners opportunities to answer questions about their own lives, give opinions, or use the *OPD* to personalize the learning process.

Following this activity are one or more content-rich contextualized exercises such as labeling, true or false, matching, sequencing, categorizing, or odd-one-out. These exercises feature an abundance of art to provide fresh, high-interest context and give essential visual support for the low-beginning learner. A variety of graphs, charts, and lifeskills documents are also provided.

As you peruse this book, you'll notice that about a third of the topics include a Challenge activity as a final exercise. Challenge activities provide higher-level critical thinking practice or additional personalization where appropriate. A standard feature in the *High Beginning* and *Low Intermediate Workbooks*, Challenge activities are introduced here to provide level-appropriate critical-thinking exercises.

Each of the 12 units ends with Another Look, a review which allows students to practice vocabulary from various topics of a unit in a game or puzzle-like activity, such as word searches, complete the picture, and P-searches, where students search a picture for items that begin with the letter p. These activities are at the back of the *Low Beginning Workbook* on pages 248–259.

Throughout the *Workbook*, vocabulary is carefully controlled and recycled. Students should, however, be encouraged to use their *Picture Dictionaries* to look up words they do not recall, or, if they are doing topics out of sequence, may not yet have learned. *The Oxford Picture Dictionary Workbooks* can be used in the classroom or at home for self-study.

Acknowledgments

The publisher and author would like to acknowledge the following individuals for their invaluable feedback during the development of this workbook:

Patricia S. Bell, Lake Technical County ESOL, FL; Patricia Castro, Harvest English Institute, NJ; Druci Diaz, CARIBE Program and TBT, FL; Jill Gluck, Hollywood Community Adult School, CA; Frances Hardenbergh, Southside Programs for Adult and Continuing Ed, VA; Mercedes Hern, Tampa, FL; (Katie) Mary C. Hurter, North Harris College, TX; Karen Kipke, Antioch Freshman Academy, TN; Ivanna Mann-Thrower, Charlotte Mecklenburg Schools, NC; Holley Mayville, Charlotte Mecklenburg Schools, NC; Jonetta Myles, Salem High School, GA; Kathleen Reynolds, Albany Park Community Center, IL; Jan Salerno, Kennedy-San Fernando CAS, CA; Jenni Santamaria, ABC Adult School, CA; Geraldyne Scott, Truman College/ Lakeview Learning Center, IL; Sharada Sekar, Antioch Freshman Academy, TN; Terry Shearer, Region IV ESC, TX; Melissa Singler, Cape Fear Community College, NC; Cynthia Wiseman, Wiseman Language Consultants, NY

Table of Contents

Introduction iii

1. Everyday Language

1.1	Meeting and Greeting	2–3
1.2	Personal Information	4
1.3	School	5
1.4	A Classroom	6–7
1.5	Studying	8–9
1.6	Succeeding in School	10
1.7	A Day at School	11
1.8	Everyday Conversation	12
1.9	Weather	13
1.10	The Telephone	14–15
1.11	Numbers	16
1.12	Measurements	17
1.13	Time	18–19
1.14	The Calendar	20–21
1.15	Calendar Events	22
1.16	Describing Things	23
1.17	Colors	24
1.18	Prepositions	25
1.19	Money	26
1.20	Shopping	27
1.21	Same and Different	28–29

2. People

2.1	Adults and Children	30–31
2.2	Describing People	32
2.3	Describing Hair	33
2.4	Families	34–35
2.5	Childcare and Parenting	36–37
2.6	Daily Routines	38–39
2.7	Life Events and Documents	40–41
2.8	Feelings	42–43
2.9	A Family Reunion	44–45

3. Housing

3.1	The Home	46–47
3.2	Finding a Home	48–49
3.3	Apartments	50–51
3.4	Different Places to Live	52
3.5	A House and Yard	53
3.6	A Kitchen	54
3.7	A Dining Area	55
3.8	A Living Room	56
3.9	A Bathroom	57
3.10	A Bedroom	58
3.11	The Kids' Bedroom	59
3.12	Housework	60
3.13	Cleaning Supplies	61
3.14	Household Problems and Repairs	62–63
3.15	The Tenant Meeting	64–65

4. Food

4.1	Back from the Market	66–67
4.2	Fruit	68
4.3	Vegetables	69
4.4	Meat and Poultry	70
4.5	Seafood and Deli	71
4.6	A Grocery Store	72–73
4.7	Containers and Packaging	74
4.8	Weights and Measurements	75
4.9	Food Preparation and Safety	76–77
4.10	Kitchen Utensils	78
4.11	A Fast Food Restaurant	79
4.12	A Coffee Shop Menu	80–81
4.13	A Restaurant	82–83
4.14	The Farmers' Market	84–85

5. Clothing

5.1	Everyday Clothes	86–87
5.2	Casual, Work, and Formal Clothes	88–89
5.3	Seasonal Clothing	90
5.4	Underwear and Sleepwear	91
5.5	Workplace Clothing	92–93
5.6	Shoes and Accessories	94–95
5.7	Describing Clothes	96–97
5.8	Making Clothes	98–99
5.9	Making Alterations	100
5.10	Doing the Laundry	101
5.11	A Garage Sale	102–103

6. Health

6.1	The Body	104–105
6.2	Inside and Outside the Body	106–107
6.3	Personal Hygiene	108–109
6.4	Symptoms and Injuries	110
6.5	Medical Care	111
6.6	Illnesses and Medical Conditions	112–113
6.7	A Pharmacy	114–115
6.8	Taking Care of Your Health	116–117
6.9	Medical Emergencies	118
6.10	First Aid	119
6.11	Dental Care	120
6.12	Health Insurance	121
6.13	A Hospital	122–123
6.14	A Health Fair	124–125

7. Community

7.1	Downtown	126–127
7.2	City Streets	128–129
7.3	An Intersection	130–131
7.4	A Mall	132–133
7.5	The Bank	134
7.6	The Library	135

Contents

7.　Community　(continued)

7.7	The Post Office	136–137
7.8	Department of Motor Vehicles (DMV)	138–139
7.9	Government and Military Service	140–141
7.10	Civic Engagement	142–143
7.11	The Legal System	144
7.12	Crime	145
7.13	Public Safety	146
7.14	Cyber Safety	147
7.15	Emergencies and Natural Disasters	148–149
7.16	Emergency Procedures	150–151
7.17	Community Cleanup	152–153

8.　Transportation

8.1	Basic Transportation	154–155
8.2	Public Transportation	156
8.3	Prepositions of Motion	157
8.4	Traffic Signs	158
8.5	Directions and Maps	159
8.6	Cars and Trucks	160
8.7	Buying and Maintaining a Car	161
8.8	Parts of a Car	162–163
8.9	An Airport	164–165
8.10	A Road Trip	166–167

9.　Job Search

9.1	Job Search	168–169
9.2	Jobs and Occupations A-C	170
9.3	Jobs and Occupations C-H	171
9.4	Jobs and Occupations H-P	172
9.5	Jobs and Occupations P-W	173
9.6	Career Planning	174–175
9.7	Job Skills	176
9.8	Office Skills	177
9.9	Soft Skills	178
9.10	Interview Skills	179
9.11	First Day on the Job	180–181

10.　The Workplace

10.1	The Workplace	182–183
10.2	Inside a Company	184
10.3	Manufacturing	185
10.4	Landscaping and Gardening	186
10.5	Farming and Ranching	187
10.6	Office Work	188–189
10.7	Information Technology (IT)	190–191
10.8	A Hotel	192
10.9	Food Service	193
10.10	Tools and Building Supplies	194–195
10.11	Construction	196
10.12	Job Safety	197
10.13	A Bad Day at Work	198–199

11. Academic Study

11.1   Schools and Subjects 200–201
11.2   English Composition 202–203
11.3   Mathematics 204–205
11.4   Science 206–207
11.5   U.S. History 208
11.6   World History 209
11.7   Digital Literacy 210–211
11.8   Internet Research 212–213
11.9   Geography and Habitats 214
11.10   The Universe 215
11.11   Trees and Plants 216
11.12   Flowers 217
11.13   Marine Life, Amphibians, and Reptiles 218–219
11.14   Birds, Insects, and Arachnids 220
11.15   Domestic Animals and Rodents 221
11.16   Mammals 222–223
11.17   Energy and the Environment 224–225
11.18   A Graduation 226–227

12. Recreation

12.1   Places to Go 228–229
12.2   The Park and Playground 230
12.3   The Beach 231
12.4   Outdoor Recreation 232
12.5   Winter and Water Sports 233
12.6   Individual Sports 234
12.7   Team Sports 235
12.8   Sports Verbs 236
12.9   Sports Equipment 237
12.10   Hobbies and Games 238–239
12.11   Electronics and Photography 240–241
12.12   Entertainment 242–243
12.13   Music 244
12.14   Holidays 245
12.15   A Birthday Party 246–247

Another Look 248–259
Verb Guide 260–262

1. Check (✓) the things you do and say every day. Look in your dictionary for help.

Word List: Meeting and Greeting

☐ Say, "Hello."   ☐ Hug.   ☐ Introduce a friend.

☐ Ask, "How are you?"   ☐ Wave.   ☐ Shake hands.

☐ Introduce yourself.   ☐ Greet people.   ☐ Kiss.

☐ Smile.   ☐ Bow.   ☐ Say, "Goodbye."

2. Complete the words. Write the letters.

a. _B_ o w.

b. K __ __ s.

c. S __ i l __.

d. G r __ __ t   p e __ p l __.

e. S __ y, "H e __ l __."

f. S __ a __ e   __ a n __ s.

g. A s __, "H __ w   a __ e   y __ __?"

h. I n __ r o d __ __ e   __ o u __ s e __ f.

3. Complete the sentences. Use the words in the box.

| bow | ~~greet~~ | hug | shake |

a. There are many ways to
   _____greet_____ people.

b. People in the United States
   _____ hands.

c. People in Japan _____.

d. People in Mexico often _____.

4. Label the picture. Write the numbers.

1. Smile.

2. Say, "Goodbye."

3. Say, "Hello."

4. Introduce a friend.

5. ~~Introduce yourself.~~

6. Wave.

5. What about you? Answer the questions.

In my country…

a. I say, "_____" to greet people.

b. I say, "_____" to introduce a friend.

In the United States…

c. I say, "_____" to greet people.

d. I say, "_____" to introduce myself.

1. Check (✓) the words you know. Look in your dictionary. Find the words you don't know.

Word List: Personal Information		
☐ say	☐ name	☐ ZIP code
☐ spell	☐ address	☐ phone number
☐ print	☐ city	☐ date of birth (DOB)
☐ type	☐ state	☐ gender
☐ sign		☐ signature

2. Match the information with the words.

  2 **a.** print   **1.** ☐ J-U-L-I-A

  ___ **b.** sign   **2.** J̶u̶l̶i̶a̶

  ___ **c.** spell   **3.** ☐ Julia

  ___ **d.** type   **4.** *Julia*

  ___ **e.** say   **5.** Ju

3. Complete the form. Use the information in the box.

Los Angeles	~~Paul Smith~~	(213) 555-9142	212 Central Avenue	male
May 7, 1962	90024	California	*Paul Smith*	

Personal Information

NAME: Paul Smith

ADDRESS:

CITY: STATE:

ZIP CODE: PHONE NUMBER:

DATE OF BIRTH: GENDER:

SIGNATURE:

1. **Check (✓) the people and places you see at school every week.**
   Look in your dictionary for help.

Word List: School		
☐ principal	☐ restrooms	☐ clerk
☐ classroom	☐ hallway	☐ cafeteria
☐ teacher	☐ main office	☐ computer lab

2. **Cross out the word that doesn't belong.**

   a. hallway ~~clerk~~ cafeteria restrooms

   b. cafeteria computer lab main office teacher

   c. clerk principal hallway teacher

   d. restrooms main office hallway principal

   e. cafeteria classroom computer lab teacher

3. **Label the picture. Write the numbers.**

   1. clerk

   2. ~~teacher~~

   3. classroom

   4. computer lab

   5. main office

   6. hallway

a. 2   b. ___   c. ___   d. ___   e. ___   f. ___

CHALLENGE Write the name of your teacher and the name of the principal at your school.

1. **Check (✓) the things you use and the things you do every day. Look in your dictionary for help.**

Word List: A Classroom		
☐ teacher	☐ pen	☐ **Listen** to a recording.
☐ student	☐ highlighter	☐ **Stand up**.
☐ desk	☐ textbook	☐ **Sit down**.
☐ chair	☐ workbook	☐ **Open** your book.
☐ computer	☐ learner's dictionary	☐ **Close** your book.
☐ pencil	☐ **Talk** to the teacher.	

2. **Cross out the word that doesn't belong.**

a. ~~chair~~   student   teacher

b. pen   highlighter   workbook

c. learner's dictionary   computer   textbook

d. desk   pencil   chair

3. **Label the picture. Write the numbers.**

1. chair	**3.** desk	**5.** pencil	**7.** textbook
2. ~~computer~~	**4.** pen	**6.** student	**8.** workbook

6

4. Label the pictures. Use the words in the box.

Talk	Close	Sit	Stand	~~Listen~~	Open

a. _____Listen_____ to the teacher.

b. _____ your textbook.

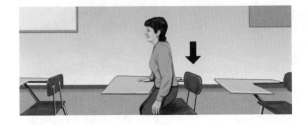

c. _____ to the students.

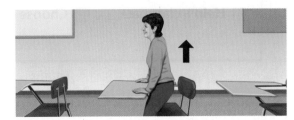

d. _____ up.

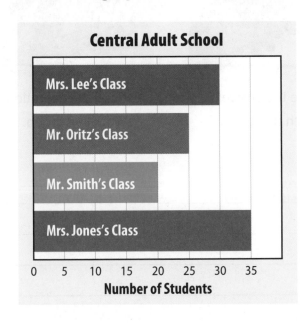

e. _____ down.

f. _____ your workbook.

5. Look at the graph. Answer the questions.

Central Adult School

Mrs. Lee's Class

Mr. Oritz's Class

Mr. Smith's Class

Mrs. Jones's Class

0 5 10 15 20 25 30 35

Number of Students

a. How many teachers are there at Central Adult School? __4__

b. How many students does Mr. Ortiz have? _____

c. How many learner's dictionaries does Mrs. Lee need for all her students? _____

d. How many desks does the school need for teachers and students? _____

1. Check (✓) the things you do with a pen or pencil. Look in your dictionary for help.

Word List: Studying

☐ **Read** the definition.   ☐ **Ask** a question.   ☐ **Circle** the answer.

☐ **Copy** the word.   ☐ **Answer** a question.   ☐ **Match** the items.

☐ **Draw** a picture.   ☐ **Share** a book.   ☐ **Take out** a piece of paper.

☐ **Work** in a group.   ☐ **Fill in** the blank.   ☐ **Put away** your books.

☐ **Help** a classmate.   ☐ **Choose** the correct answer.

---

2. Look at the pictures. Check (✓) the correct sentences.

a.

☐ Put away your books.
✓ Share a book.

b.

☐ Ask a question.
☐ Copy the word.

c.

☐ Draw a picture.
☐ Answer a question.

d.

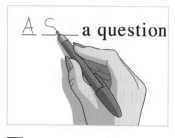

☐ Choose the answer.
☐ Fill in the blank.

e.

☐ Circle the answer.
☐ Match the items.

f.

☐ Read the definition.
☐ Work in a group.

3. Unscramble the sentences.

a. definition. the Read   _Read the definition._

b. your away Put books.   _____

c. classmate. Help a   _____

d. out a paper. piece Take of _____

e. blank. in the Fill   _____

4. Take the test.

A. Circle the correct words.

1. Help a (classmate) / picture.

2. Read the blank / definition.

3. Choose the correct answer / piece of paper.

B. Copy the words.

1. share _____share_____

2. choose _____

3. ask _____

4. answer _____

C. Match the words.

_3_ a. Draw   1. the blank.

____ b. Fill in   2. in a group.

____ c. Put away   3. a picture.

____ d. Work   4. your books.

D. Read the story. Circle the words from the Word List on page 8.

I like my English class very much. Every day I (work in a group). I share a book with my classmate. We read stories and answer questions together. Then we put away our books and speak English.

5. What about you? Answer the questions. Write *Yes, I do* or *No, I don't.*

a. Do you like to work in a group?   _____.

b. Do you share a book every day?   _____.

c. Do you ask many questions in class? _____.

d. Do you like to draw pictures?   _____.

9

1. Check (✓) the words you know. Look in your dictionary. Find the words you don't know.

Word List: Succeeding in School		
☐ **Set** goals.	☐ **Bubble in** the answer.	☐ test booklet
☐ **Take** notes.	☐ **Check** your work.	☐ answer sheet
☐ **Study** at home.	☐ **Correct** the mistake.	
☐ **Ask** for help.	☐ **Hand in** your test.	

2. Look at the pictures. Put the sentences in order (1–6).

1.
2.
3.
4.
5.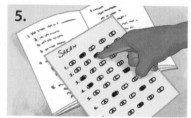
6.

___ Open your test booklet.

_1_ Write your name on the answer sheet.

___ Check your work.

___ Ask for help.

___ Hand in your test.

___ Bubble in the answers.

3. Complete the story. Use the words in the box.

help	home	~~notes~~	set	check	correct

a. I take _____notes_____ in English class every day.

b. Sometimes I ask my teacher for _____ .

c. I study at _____ in the evening.

d. I always _____ my work.

e. Then I _____ the mistakes.

f. I like to _____ goals. They help me study.

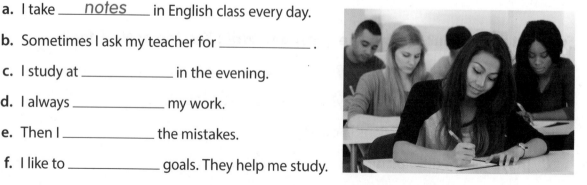

1. Check (✓) the things your teacher does every day. Look in your dictionary for help.

Word List: A Day at School

☐ **Walk** to class.   ☐ **Take** a break.   ☐ **Have** a conversation.

☐ **Enter** the room.   ☐ **Eat**.   ☐ **Leave** the room.

☐ **Turn on** the lights.   ☐ **Drink**.   ☐ **Turn off** the lights.

2. Read the poster. Write *T* (true) or *F* (false).

a. Students cannot eat in the classroom. _T_

b. Students can drink water in class. ___

c. The teacher turns off all the computers. ___

d. Students take a break every school day. ___

e. Students leave the room to eat and drink. ___

f. The rules say to enter the room quietly. ___

Computer Class Student Rules 🖥️

1. Do not eat or drink in class.

2. Turn off your computer every day.

3. Break time is 10:15 – 10:30.

4. Enter and leave the room quietly.

3. Complete the crossword puzzle.

ACROSS

2. ___ on the computer.

4. ___ water.

5. Take a ___.

8. Turn ___ the lights.

DOWN

1. Have a ___.

3. ___ to class.

6. Leave the ___.

7. ___ a snack.

		¹			
²T	U	R	N		³
		⁴			
⁵	⁶				⁷
		⁸			

1. Check (✓) the things you hear people say every day. Look in your dictionary for help.

> ### Word List: Everyday Conversation
>
> ☐ **start** a conversation
> *Tell me about . . .*
>
> ☐ **thank** someone
> *Thank you very much.*
>
> ☐ **offer** something
> *Here. Use my pen.*
>
> ☐ **refuse** an offer
> *No, thanks. I have one.*
>
> ☐ **apologize**
> *I'm sorry.*
>
> ☐ **accept** an apology
> *That's OK.*
>
> ☐ **agree**
> *This is a great movie.*
> *Yes, it is.*
>
> ☐ **disagree**
> *This is a bad movie.*
> *No! It's great!*

2. Match the sentences.

_2_ **a.** I'm sorry.

___ **b.** Tell me about your children.

___ **c.** This is a good book.

___ **d.** Here. Use my highlighter.

___ **e.** This is a bad movie.

1. Yes, it is.

2. ~~That's OK.~~

3. No! It's good!

4. They're great.

5. No, thanks.

3. Label the pictures. Write the numbers.

_2_ **a.**  ___ **b.**  ___ **c.**

___ **d.**  ___ **e.**  ___ **f.**

1. accept an apology

2. ~~agree~~

3. apologize

4. disagree

5. start a conversation

6. thank someone

1. Check (✓) the words that describe the weather this week. Look in your dictionary for help.

Word List: Weather		
☐ hot	☐ cold	☐ rain
☐ warm	☐ sunny	☐ snow
☐ cool	☐ cloudy	☐ windy

2. Look at the map. Write *T* (true) or *F* (false).

a. It's hot in Los Angeles. _T_

b. It's cold in Dallas. ___

c. It's cool in New York. ___

d. It's warm in Miami. ___

e. It's snowing in Los Angeles. ___

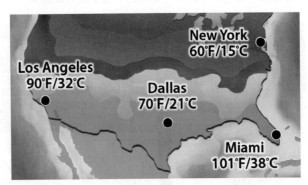

New York
60°F/15°C

Los Angeles
90°F/32°C

Dallas
70°F/21°C

Miami
101°F/38°C

3. Look at the weather forecast. Use the words in the box to describe the weather for each day.

cloudy	raining	~~sunny~~	snowing	windy

Five-Day Forecast for Denver

a. Monday	b. Tuesday	c. Wednesday	d. Thursday	e. Friday
70°	61°	42°	34°	60°

a. _sunny_ and warm b. _____ and cool c. _____ and cold d. _____ and cold e. _____ and cool

CHALLENGE Write three words that describe your favorite weather.

1. Check (✓) the things you use every day. Look in your dictionary for help.

Word List: The Telephone		
☐ receiver	☐ charger cord	☐ missed call
☐ keypad	☐ charger plug	☐ voice mail
☐ star key	☐ contact list	☐ text message
☐ pound key	☐ cell phone	

2. Label the picture. Write the numbers.

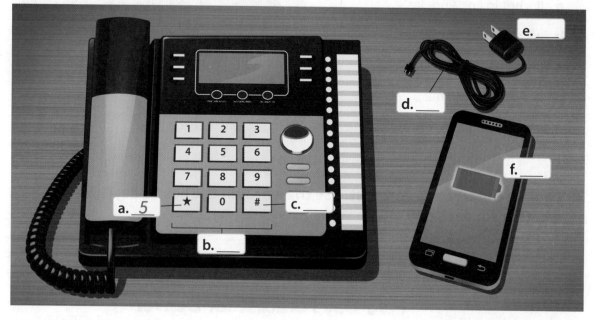

a. _5_
b. ____
c. ____
d. ____
e. ____
f. ____

1. cell phone	**3.** charger plug	**5.** ~~star key~~
2. pound key	**4.** keypad	**6.** charger cord

3. Complete the sentences. Use the words in the box.

contact	~~missed~~	voice mail	text

a. Marta has one ___*missed*___ call.

b. The name is not in her _____ list. Who is it?

c. She listens to the _____. It's from a classmate.

d. She sends her classmate a _____ message.

4. **Check (✓) the words you know. Look in your dictionary. Find the words you don't know.**

Word List: The Telephone	
☐ area code	☐ **Dial** the phone number.
☐ phone number	☐ **Press** "talk."
☐ local call	☐ **Talk** on the phone.
☐ long-distance call	☐ **Hang up**.
☐ international call	☐ **Dial** 911.

5. **Match the numbers with the words.**

    _3_ **a.** 54-2-555-1931   **1.** area code

    ___ **b.** (714)   **2.** long-distance call

    ___ **c.** 555-2682   **3.** ~~international call~~

    ___ **d.** (714) 555-2682   **4.** emergency call

    ___ **e.** 911   **5.** local call

6. **Tom is making a phone call. Put the sentences in order (1–5).**

    ___ **a.** Talk on the phone.

    ___ **b.** Dial the phone number.

    ___ **c.** Hang up.

    _1_ **d.** Dial the area code.

    ___ **e.** Press "talk."

Numbers

1. Write the number next to the word. Look in your dictionary for help.

Word List: Numbers

one	_1_	eleven	___	twenty-one	___
two	___	twelve	___	thirty	___
three	___	thirteen	___	forty	___
four	___	fourteen	___	fifty	___
five	___	fifteen	___	sixty	___
six	___	sixteen	___	seventy	___
seven	___	seventeen	___	eighty	___
eight	___	eighteen	___	ninety	___
nine	___	nineteen	___	one hundred	___
ten	___	twenty	___		

2. Study the chart. Complete the sentences. Use the words in the box.

Twenty-five	~~Fifty~~	Seventy-five	One hundred

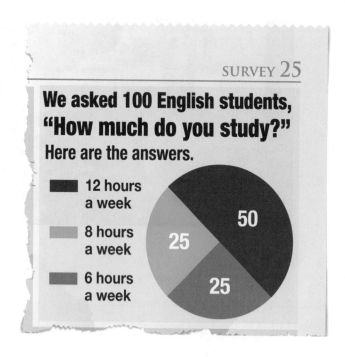

SURVEY 25

We asked 100 English students, "How much do you study?"
Here are the answers.

- 12 hours a week
- 8 hours a week
- 6 hours a week

50 · 25 · 25

a. _____ _Fifty_ _____
   students study 12 hours a week.

b. _____
   students study 8 hours a week.

c. _____
   students study 6 hours or more.

d. _____
   students study 8 hours or more.

CHALLENGE   How many hours a week do you study?

16

1. Check (✓) the words you know. Look in your dictionary. Find the words you don't know.

Word List: Measurements		

Fractions
- ☐ one whole (1)
- ☐ one half (1/2)
- ☐ one fourth (1/4)

Percents
- ☐ 100 percent (100%)
- ☐ 50 percent (50%)
- ☐ 25 percent (25%)

Measurements
- ☐ inch (in.)
- ☐ height
- ☐ length

2. Write *T* (true) or *F* (false).

<u>T</u> **a.** one whole = 100%

___ **b.** 50% = one fourth

___ **c.** 1/4 = 25 percent

___ **d.** 50 percent + 50 percent = 100%

___ **e.** one half = 25%

___ **f.** 1/4 + 1/4 = one whole

3. Look at the picture. Circle the correct words.

a. (Fifty percent) / Seventy-five percent of the students are men.

b. One fourth / One half of the students are with the teacher.

c. Fifty percent / One hundred percent of the students are at the whiteboard.

d. The length / height of the table is 36 inches.

e. The woman is measuring the length / height of the table.

f. The length of the table is 48 inches / percent.

Time

1. Check (✓) the words you know. Look in your dictionary. Find the words you don't know.

Word List: Time		
☐ hour	☐ 1:00 (one o'clock)	☐ morning
☐ minutes	☐ 1:15 (one-fifteen)	☐ afternoon
☐ seconds	☐ 1:30 (one-thirty)	☐ evening
☐ a.m.	☐ 1:45 (one-forty-five)	☐ night
☐ p.m.		

2. Match the pictures with the times.

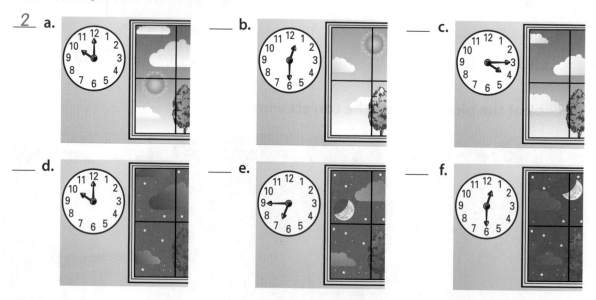

_2_ a.   ___ b.   ___ c.

___ d.   ___ e.   ___ f.

1. It's 12:30 p.m.

2. ~~It's 10:00 in the morning.~~

3. It's 4:15 in the afternoon.

4. It's 12:30 a.m.

5. It's 10:00 at night.

6. It's 6:45 in the evening.

3. Complete the sentences. Use the words in the box.

hours	minutes	a.m.	~~seconds~~	p.m.	time

a. There are 60 ___seconds___ in a minute.

b. There are 60 _____ in an hour.

c. There are 24 _____ in a day.

d. What _____ is it?

e. Good morning. It's 7:30 _____.

f. It's 10:00 _____. Good night.

4. Check (✓) your time zone. Look in your dictionary for help.

Word List: Time
☐ early   ☐ Pacific time   ☐ Central time
☐ on time   ☐ Mountain time   ☐ Eastern time
☐ late

5. Unscramble the words.

a. n o m e i t   <u>o</u> n t <u>i</u> <u>m</u> <u>e</u>

b. a e l t   l __ t __

c. l e y a r   e __ __ __ y

d. t r a l n e C   C __ __ t __ __ l

e. s t e a E n r   E __ __ __ __ __ n

f. c i f c i P a   P __ __ __ f __ __

6. Label the map. Use the words in the box.

Eastern time	Central time	Mountain time	~~Pacific time~~

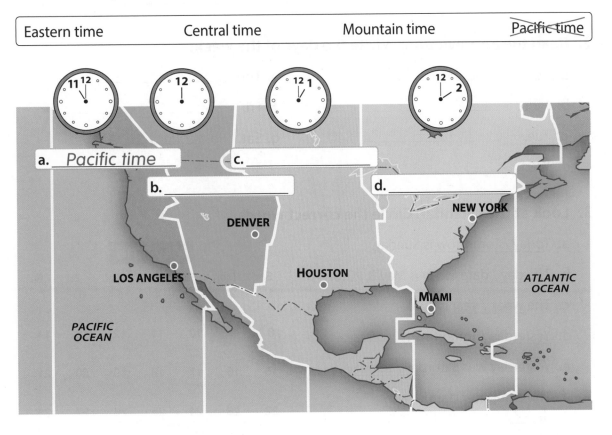

a. _Pacific time_

b. _____

c. _____

d. _____

NEW YORK

DENVER

LOS ANGELES

HOUSTON

MIAMI

ATLANTIC OCEAN

PACIFIC OCEAN

The Calendar

1. **Check (✓) the words you know. Look in your dictionary. Find the words you don't know.**

Word List: The Calendar	
	Days of the Week
☐ date	☐ Sunday
☐ day	☐ Monday
☐ month	☐ Tuesday
☐ year	☐ Wednesday
☐ today	☐ Thursday
☐ tomorrow	☐ Friday
☐ yesterday	☐ Saturday

2. **Read the abbreviations. Write the days of the week.**

    a. Sun. _____Sunday_____   e. Thu. _____

    b. Mon. _____   f. Fri. _____

    c. Tue. _____   g. Sat. _____

    d. Wed. _____

3. **Look at the calendar. Circle the correct words.**

    a. (Today) / Tomorrow is Sunday.

    b. The <u>day / date</u> today is May 8, 2016.

    c. The <u>week / year</u> is 2016.

    d. <u>Yesterday / Tomorrow</u> is Monday.

    e. Yesterday was <u>Saturday / Sunday</u>.

    f. The computer class is two
       <u>days / months</u> every week.

    g. The <u>date / month</u> is May.

May 2016						
Sun	Mon	Tue	Wed	Thu	Fri	Sat
1	2	3 computer class	4	5 computer class	6	7
8	9	10 computer class	11	12 computer class	13	14
15	16	17 computer class	18	19 computer class	20	21
22	23	24 computer class	25	26 computer class	27	28
29	30	31 computer class				

4. Read the months. Write the abbreviations. Look in your dictionary for help.

Word List: The Calendar

Months of the Year

January	_Jan._	May	_____	September	_____
February	_____	June	_____	October	_____
March	_____	July	_____	November	_____
April	_____	August	_____	December	_____

---

5. Complete the chart with the months of the year.

Spring	Summer	Fall	Winter
March	June	September	_____
April	July	_____	January
May	_____	_____	_____

6. Write the dates.

a. 03/12/ 01   _March 12, 2001_   d. 07/07/14 _____

b. 09/25/04 _____   e. 02/01/18 _____

c. 05/16/07 _____   f. 06/30/21 _____

7. Look at the chart. Write _T_ (true) or _F_ (false).

a. It's cold in Fargo in January.   _T_

b. It's hot in Chicago in April.   ____

c. It's hot in Hawaii in October.   ____

d. It's hot in Houston in July.   ____

e. It's cold in Fargo in July.   ____

How's the Weather?

CITY	Jan.	Apr.	Jul.	Oct.
Fargo, North Dakota ▶	7°	43°	70°	45°
Chicago, Illinois ▶	22°	48°	73°	52°
Houston, Texas ▶	52°	69°	84°	70°
Honolulu, Hawaii ▶	73°	76°	81°	80°

Calendar Events

1. Check (✓) the things you celebrate every year. Look in your dictionary for help.

> ### Word List: Calender Events
>
> ☐ birthday   ☐ Presidents' Day   ☐ Columbus Day
>
> ☐ appointment   ☐ Memorial Day   ☐ Veterans Day
>
> ☐ New Year's Day   ☐ Fourth of July   ☐ Thanksgiving
>
> ☐ Martin Luther King Jr. Day   ☐ Labor Day   ☐ Christmas

2. Match the holidays with the months.

_3_ **a.** Martin Luther King Jr. Day   **1.** October

____ **b.** Presidents' Day   **2.** May

____ **c.** Memorial Day   **3.** ~~January~~

____ **d.** Labor Day   **4.** December

____ **e.** Columbus Day   **5.** February

____ **f.** Christmas   **6.** September

3. Label the pictures. Use the words in the box.

Veterans Day   Fourth of July   ~~birthday~~   New Year's Day   appointment   Thanksgiving

a. _____ *birthday* _____   b. _____   c. _____

d. _____   e. _____   f. _____

1. Check (✓) the words that describe this book. Look in your dictionary for help.

Word List: Describing Things

☐ little   ☐ bad   ☐ beautiful

☐ big   ☐ good   ☐ ugly

☐ fast   ☐ expensive   ☐ easy

☐ slow   ☐ cheap   ☐ difficult

2. Write the opposite words. Use the words in the box.

~~big~~   bad   difficult   beautiful   slow   expensive

a. little   _____big_____   **d.** good   _____

b. cheap   _____   **e.** ugly   _____

c. easy   _____   **f.** fast   _____

3. Look at the picture. Circle the correct words.

a. The TV is (big) / little.

b. It's expensive / cheap.

c. The picture is good / bad.

d. They think the TV is ugly / beautiful.

e. It's easy / difficult to see the picture on the TV.

4. What about you? Answer the questions.

a. Is your classroom big or little?   _____

b. Is your class easy or difficult?   _____

c. Is the news on TV today good or bad?   _____

Colors

1. Check (✓) the colors you see in your classroom. Look in your dictionary for help.

Word List: Colors			
☐ red	☐ orange	☐ pink	☐ white
☐ yellow	☐ green	☐ black	☐ brown
☐ blue	☐ purple		

2. Match the words with the colors.

_4_ **a.** black   ___ **c.** brown   ___ **e.** orange   ___ **g.** purple   ___ **i.** white

___ **b.** blue   ___ **d.** green   ___ **f.** pink   ___ **h.** red   ___ **j.** yellow

1. ☐   3. ☐   5. ☐   7. ☐   9. ☐

2. ☐   4. ■   6. ☐   8. ☐   10. ☐

3. Look at the picture. Read the sentences. Number the people.

a. _5_   c. ____   b. ____   d. ____   e. ____   f. ____

1. Lee has a red pen and a yellow book.   4. Sue has a pink and white book.

2. Ned has a black pen and a red book.   5. ~~Tim has a blue book and an orange book~~.

3. Won has a purple book and a green pen.   6. Maria has a brown book and a green book.

[CHALLENGE]   Name 2 colors you see on the front of this workbook.

1. Check (✓) the words you can use to make a true sentence, "There's a book ____ my desk." Look in your dictionary for help.

Word List: Prepositions		
☐ above	☐ in front of	☐ under
☐ below	☐ behind	☐ on
☐ in	☐ next to	☐ between

2. Unscramble the words.

a. b e d h i n   b _e_ _h_ i _n_ d   **d.** b e w o l   b __ l o __

b. b e n w e e t   b __ t w __ __ n   **e.** t e x n t o   n __ __ __ __ t __

c. u d r e n   u n __ __ r   **f.** a v e b o   a __ o __ __

3. Look at the picture. Write *T* (true) or *F* (false).

a. There's a book on the table.   _T_

b. The red book is next to the blue book.   ___

c. The man is sitting in front of the chair.   ___

d. There's a book under the table.   ___

e. The green book is above the red book.   ___

f. The blue book is between the red book and the black book.   ___

g. The table is behind the books.   ___

h. The blue book is below the black book.   ___

Money

1. **Check (✓) the money you have with you today. Look in your dictionary for help.**

Word List: Money		
☐ a penny	☐ a quarter	☐ ten dollars
☐ a nickel	☐ a dollar	☐ twenty dollars
☐ a dime	☐ five dollars	☐ one hundred dollars

2. **Match the words with the numbers.**

_5_ **a.** a penny   **1.** 5¢

___ **b.** a nickel   **2.** 10¢

___ **c.** a dime   **3.** 25¢

___ **d.** a quarter   **4.** $10.00

___ **e.** a dollar   **5.** ~~1¢~~

___ **f.** ten dollars   **6.** $1.00

3. **Look at the pictures. How much money do you see? Write the answers.**

a. ____25¢____   b. _____   c. _____   d. _____

e. _____   f. _____   g. _____   h. _____

CHALLENGE   Look at the pictures in Exercise 3. What is the total of all the money?

26

1. Check (✓) the words you know. Look in your dictionary. Find the words you don't know.

Word List: Shopping		
☐ **pay** cash	☐ **write** a check	☐ price
☐ **use** a credit card	☐ **buy**	☐ sales tax
☐ **use** a debit card	☐ receipt	☐ total

2. Study the receipt. Circle the correct words.

a. This is a customer's (receipt) / credit card for Brown's Books.

b. The total / sales tax is $2.79.

c. The check / price of one English textbook is $19.00.

d. The tax / total of the receipt is $34.78.

e. The customer pays with a credit card / cash.

```
-------------------------------------
   BROWN'S  BOOKS
      221 FIRST AVENUE
-------------------------------------

ITEM                      PRICE
1 ENGLISH TEXTBOOK @    $19.00
1 ENGLISH WORKBOOK @    $12.99

SUBTOTAL                $31.99
SALES TAX               $ 2.79
TOTAL                   $34.78

PAYMENT METHOD:         CASH
```

3. Study the chart. Complete the sentences. Use the words in the box.

cash	write	buy	credit	Fifteen	~~pay~~	debit

a. Thirty-two percent of people like to ____pay____ cash.

b. Thirty-one percent like to use _____ cards.

c. _____ percent like to _____ checks.

d. Most people pay _____ or use debit cards to buy things.

e. Twenty-two percent like to use _____ cards.

f. How do you like to _____ things?

Ways People Buy Things in the U.S.

32% cash
15% check
31% debit
22% credit

27

Same and Different

1. Check (✓) the words you know. Look in your dictionary. Find the words
   you don't know.

Word List: Same and Different			
☐ twins	☐ matching	☐ navy blue	☐ **shop**
☐ sweater	☐ disappointed	☐ happy	☐ **keep**

2. Look at the pictures. Write *T* (true) or *F* (false).

a. Danny is disappointed.   _F_

b. His sweater is navy blue.   ___

c. He likes the sweater.
   He wants to keep it.   ___

d. Alex is disappointed.   ___

e. He likes the sweater.   ___

f. He's happy. He wants
   to keep the sweater.   ___

g. The boys are twins.   ___

h. They're shopping with
   their mother.   ___

i. They're happy.   ___

3. Look at the pictures. Circle the correct words.

a. Mary and Sue Jones
   are (twins)/ disappointed.

b. They're <u>shopping</u> / matching
   with their mother.

c. Mary likes to <u>match</u> / <u>shop</u>.
   She's <u>disappointed</u> / <u>happy</u>.

d. Sue isn't <u>happy</u> / <u>disappointed</u>.
   She doesn't like to shop.
   She wants to go to the park.

e. Mrs. Jones buys <u>happy</u> / <u>matching</u>
   sweaters for the girls.

f. The sweaters are <u>navy blue</u> / <u>green</u>.

g. They go to the park. Now
   everybody is <u>happy</u> / <u>different</u>.

4. What about you? Answer the questions.

a. Do you like to shop? _____

b. What colors do you like? _____

Adults and Children

1. Check (✓) the people you see in your class. Look in your dictionary for help.

Word List: Adults and Children		
☐ man	☐ senior citizen	☐ 6-year-old boy
☐ woman	☐ infant	☐ 10-year-old girl
☐ women	☐ baby	☐ teenager
☐ men	☐ toddler	

2. Cross out the word that doesn't belong.

a. babies   infants   ~~man~~

b. 6-year-old boy   ~~woman~~   baby boy

c. infant   men   women

d. baby girl   senior citizen   toddler

e. woman   baby   man

f. teenager   16-year-old girl   infant

3. Label the pictures. Use the words in the box.

~~teenager~~   infant   toddler   senior citizen   6-year-old boy   man

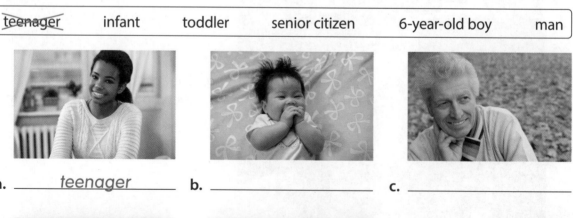

a. _*teenager*_

b. _____

c. _____

d. _____

e. _____

f. _____

4. Complete the crossword puzzle.

		²							
¹M	A	N							
							⁵		
				⁴					
		³							
			⁶						

ACROSS

1. John is 40 years old.
   He's a ___.

3. Armando is 16.
   He's a ___.

6. Ivan is 7 years old. Tom is 9.
   They're ___.

DOWN

2. Paulo is six months old.
   He's an ___.

4. Patricia is 74 years old.
   She's a ___ citizen.

5. Amanda is 25. Gloria is 27.
   They're ___.

5. Study the chart. Complete the sentences.

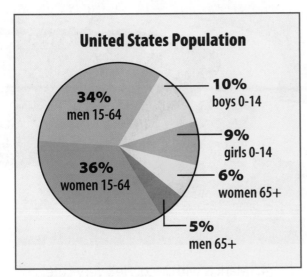

Based on information from: US. Census Bureau, American Fact Finder 2014.

a. Nineteen percent of the population are boys and ___*girls*___ .

b. _____ percent of the population are women ages 15–64.

c. _____ percent of the population are senior citizens.

d. Seventy percent of the population are _____ and _____ 15–64 years old.

e. _____ percent of the population is female.

Describing People

1. Check (✓) the words that describe your friends. Look in your dictionary for help.

Word List: Describing People		
☐ young	☐ short	☐ attractive
☐ elderly	☐ heavy	☐ cute
☐ tall	☐ thin	☐ pregnant

2. Unscramble the words.

a. latl   t a _l_ _l_

b. thni   t __ __ n

c. etuc   c __ t __

d. storh   s __ __ __ t

e. ygoun   y __ __ n __

f. veahy   h e __ __ __

g. grepannt   p r __ g __ __ __ t

h. ettraictav   __ t t __ __ __ t __ v __

3. Look at the picture. Read the sentences. Number the people.

1. Carlos is tall and thin. He's elderly.

2. ~~Jim is a young man. He's tall.~~

3. Nora is attractive. She's with Jim.

4. Mark is with Meg. He's very cute.

5. Meg is a thin, elderly woman.

6. Joanne is pregnant. She is Mark's mother.

1. **Check (✓) the words that describe your hair. Look in your dictionary for help.**

Word List: Describing Hair		
☐ short hair	☐ curly hair	☐ blond hair
☐ long hair	☐ black hair	☐ brown hair
☐ straight hair	☐ red hair	☐ gray hair

2. **Complete the sentences. Use the words in the box.**

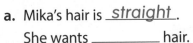

long   ~~straight~~   curly   gray   short   brown

a. Mika's hair is _straight_ .
She wants _____ hair.

b. Wilma's hair is _____.
She wants _____ hair.

c. Al's hair is _____.
He wants _____ hair.

3. **Look at the graph. Write _T_ (true) or _F_ (false).**

a. Eight students have gray hair. _T_

b. Two students have red hair. ___

c. Twenty students have black or brown hair. ___

d. No students have red hair. ___

e. Seven students have blond hair. ___

f. Sixteen students have brown hair. ___

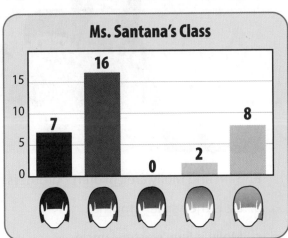

Ms. Santana's Class

Families

1. Check (✓) the people you talk to every week. Look in your dictionary for help.

Word List: Families

☐ grandmother   ☐ brother   ☐ husband

☐ grandfather   ☐ aunt   ☐ daughter

☐ mother   ☐ uncle   ☐ son

☐ father   ☐ cousin

☐ sister   ☐ wife

2. Complete the words. Write the letters.

Men and Boys

a. g r __ __ d __ __ t h __ r

b. f a __ __ e r

c. __ n c l __

d. b r o __ __ e r

e. s __ __

f. __ __ __ b __ __ __

Women and Girls

a. g r _a_ n d _m_ o t _h_ e r

b. m o t h e __

c. a u __ __

d. __ __ s __ e __

e. d __ __ __ __ __ __ r

f. __ i f __

3. Look at the picture. Circle the correct words.

a. Sam and Molly are (children) / brothers.

b. Liz is their sister / mother.

c. Molly is Sam's sister / uncle.

d. Liz and David are children / parents.

e. Sam is David and Liz's cousin / son.

f. David is Molly's father / brother.

4. Read the sentences. Label the people in the picture.

My name is Alicia. My husband is Alfred.

We have two daughters. Their names are Tina and Michelle.

Tina is married to Matt. They have one son. His name is Tony.

Michelle is married to Bill. They have a boy and a girl.

Their son is Dan. Their daughter is Emily.

a. _____ b. ____Alfred____

c. _____ d. _____ e. _____ f. _____

g. _____ h. _____ i. _____

5. Look at the pictures in Exercise 4. Write *T* (true) or *F* (false).

a. Bill is Tina's husband. ___F___   d. Bill and Michelle are parents. _____

b. Alicia is a grandmother. _____   e. Tina and Matt are brother and sister. _____

c. Tina and Michelle are sisters. _____   f. Tony and Emily are cousins. _____

CHALLENGE   Make a family tree.

1. Check (✓) five great ways to help a baby sleep. Look in your dictionary for help.

Word List: Childcare and Parenting			
☐ **hold**	☐ **bathe**	☐ **play** with	☐ **sing** a lullaby
☐ **feed**	☐ **change** a diaper	☐ **read** to	☐ **kiss** goodnight

2. Look at the pictures. Circle the correct words.

a. Hi. I'm Luis. This is my son, Sam.
I (hold) / bathe Sam and feed / kiss
him every morning.

b. I change a diaper / play with Sam.

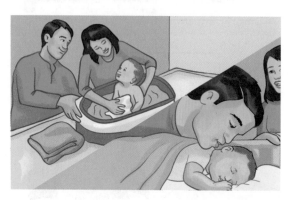

c. In the evening my wife and I
bathe / read to Sam. Then we
kiss / feed him goodnight.

d. Oh, and one more thing! We
bathe / change diapers all day and
all night.

3. What about you? Answer the questions. Write *Yes, I do* or *No, I don't.*

a. Do you like to play with children? _____

b. Do you like to read to children? _____

c. Do you like to sing to children? _____

d. Do you like to change diapers? _____

4. **Check (✓) the things you have in your home. Look in your dictionary for help.**

Word List: Childcare and Parenting			
☐ bottle	☐ baby food	☐ diaper	☐ wipes
☐ formula	☐ high chair	☐ diaper bag	☐ stroller

5. **Label the picture. Use the words in the box.**

bottles	high chair	diapers	wipes	~~diaper bag~~	stroller

b. _____

c. _____

a. *diaper bag*

d. _____

e. _____

f. _____

6. **Look at the budget. Answer the questions.**

Baby Budget

Item	Formula		
Cost per Week	$21.00	$16.00	$9.00

a. How much does baby food cost every month? $64.00

b. How much do diapers cost every month?   _____

c. How much does formula cost every day?   _____

d. How much do formula and diapers cost every week?   _____

e. How much do formula, baby food, and diapers cost every month?   _____

Daily Routines

1. **Check (✓) the things you do every morning. Look in your dictionary for help.**

Word List: Daily Routines			
☐ **get up**	☐ **get dressed**	☐ **make** lunch	☐ **be** in class
☐ **take** a shower	☐ **eat** breakfast	☐ **drive** to work	☐ **work**

2. **Unscramble the sentences.**

a. We morning. breakfast every eat   *We eat breakfast every morning.*

b. She at gets 7:00. up   _____

c. I to in 11:00. am from class 8:00   _____

d. Joe shower takes every a day.   _____

e. They at make lunch noon.   _____

3. **Look at the pictures. Complete the routine. Use the words in the box.**

drive to work   get dressed   eat breakfast   work   ~~get up~~   take a shower

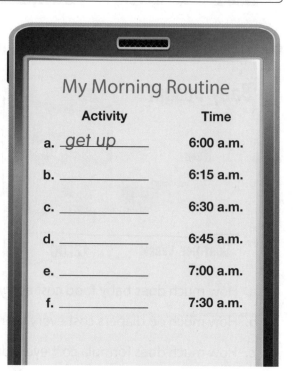

My Morning Routine

Activity	Time
a. *get up*	6:00 a.m.
b. _____	6:15 a.m.
c. _____	6:30 a.m.
d. _____	6:45 a.m.
e. _____	7:00 a.m.
f. _____	7:30 a.m.

CHALLENGE How long does it take the man to drive to work?

4. Check (✓) the things you do every evening. Look in your dictionary for help.

Word List: Daily Routines		
☐ **clean** the house	☐ **come** home	☐ **read** the paper
☐ **exercise**	☐ **have** dinner	☐ **watch** TV
☐ **cook** dinner	☐ **do** homework	☐ **go** to bed

5. Look at the pictures. Put the sentences in order (1–6).

____ They do homework.

____ They go to bed.

____ They clean and cook dinner.

____ They exercise and watch TV.

____ They have dinner.

_1_ They come home.

6. Write your evening routine. Look in your dictionary for help.

My Evening Routine

Activity	Time

1. Check (✓) events from your life and documents you have. Look in your dictionary for help.

Word List: Life Events and Documents

☐ **be born**　　　　☐ **get** married　　　☐ birth certificate

☐ **start** school　　☐ **have** a baby　　　☐ diploma

☐ **immigrate**　　　☐ **buy** a home　　　☐ Social Security card

☐ **graduate**　　　　☐ **retire**　　　　　☐ passport

☐ **get** a job　　　　☐ **travel**

☐ **become** a citizen　☐ **die**

2. Complete the words. Write the letters.

a. g _e_ t a _j_ o _b_

b. b __ __ b __ __ __ __

c. s t __ __ __ t s __ __ __ o o __

d. b e __ o __ __ __ __ a c __ __ __ i __ e n

e. __ u y a h __ __ __ __

f. h __ __ e a __ __ __ __ y

3. Look at the pictures. Circle the correct words.

a. Raj and Dhara get / (have) a new baby. The baby needs a birth certificate / diploma.

b. Lin graduates / buys a house today. She's getting her Social Secrity card / diploma.

c. There's a party for Leticia today. She's going to graduate / retire soon.

d. Frank has a new passport / diploma. Now he can travel / buy a home.

4. Label the pictures. Write the numbers.

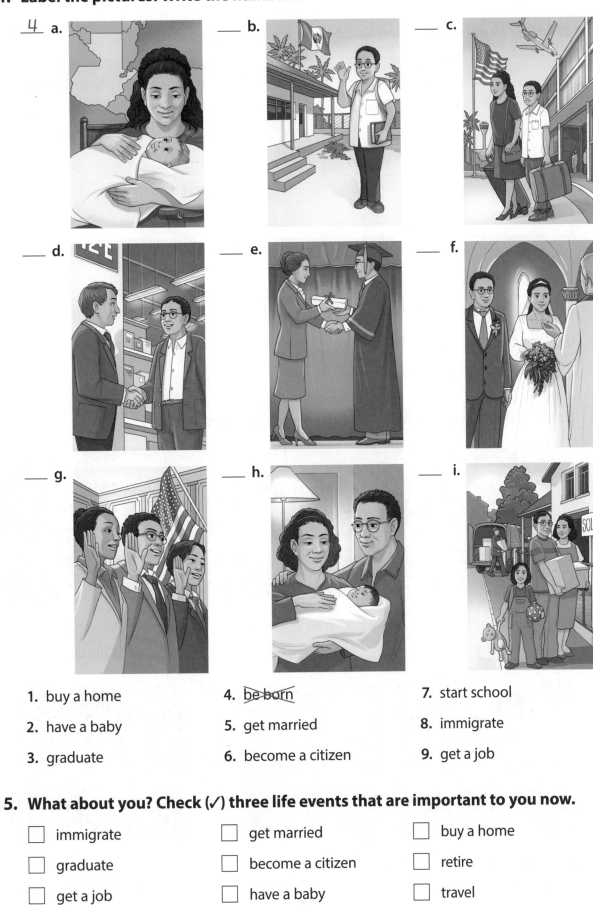

__4__ a.

___ b.

___ c.

___ d.

___ e.

___ f.

___ g.

___ h.

___ i.

1. buy a home

2. have a baby

3. graduate

4. ~~be born~~

5. get married

6. become a citizen

7. start school

8. immigrate

9. get a job

5. What about you? Check (✓) three life events that are important to you now.

☐ immigrate

☐ graduate

☐ get a job

☐ get married

☐ become a citizen

☐ have a baby

☐ buy a home

☐ retire

☐ travel

Feelings

1. **Check (✓) how you feel today. Look in your dictionary for help.**

Word List: Feelings

☐ hot	☐ uncomfortable	☐ relieved	☐ angry
☐ thirsty	☐ sick	☐ sad	☐ happy
☐ cold	☐ worried	☐ excited	☐ tired
☐ hungry	☐ well	☐ bored	

2. **Cross out the word that doesn't belong.**

a. ~~happy~~   hot   thirsty   d. angry   well   uncomfortable

b. sick   excited   tired   e. bored   tired   relieved

c. happy   excited   cold

3. **Look at the pictures. Check (✓) the correct sentences.**

a. ✓ She's thirsty.
   ☐ She's bored.

b. ☐ They're angry.
   ☐ They're sick.

c. ☐ He's angry.
   ☐ He's hungry.

d. ☐ They're worried.
   ☐ They're happy.

e. ☐ They're excited.
   ☐ They're cold.

f. ☐ He's sad. She's tired.
   ☐ She's tired. He's happy.

4. Look at the picture. Read the sentences. Number the people.

a. _5_
b. ____
c. ____
d. ____
e. ___
f. ___

1. Wilma is worried. She thinks her test is bad.

2. Henry is hungry. He needs lunch.

3. Tran is tired. He worked last night.

4. Raul is relieved. His test is good.

5. ~~Carol is cold. She needs a sweater.~~

6. Erica is happy. Her test is excellent.

5. Read the paragraph. Circle the words that describe feelings.

Today is the first day of English class. How do the students feel? A lot of students are (excited) about class. Some students are worried about speaking English. Other students are relieved because the class is not too difficult. Many students are happy because they like the teacher. Two students are bored. They need to change levels. Three students are sick. They aren't at school today.

CHALLENGE Write three words that describe your feelings on the first day of class.

A Family Reunion

1. Check (✓) the words you know. Look in your dictionary. Find the words you don't know.

Word List: A Family Reunion			
☐ banner	☐ opinion	☐ glad	☐ **laugh**
☐ baseball game	☐ balloons	☐ relatives	☐ **misbehave**

2. Match the words with the pictures.

<u>5</u> **a.** baseball game   ___ **c.** relatives   ___ **e.** banner

___ **b.** laugh   ___ **d.** misbehave   ___ **f.** balloons

1.

2.

3.

4.

5.

6.

3. Look at the pictures. Circle the correct words.

a. The Garcia family is having (a reunion)/ a baseball game.

b. Many of Cesar Garcia's <u>opinions / relatives</u> are here today.

c. Cesar is <u>misbehaving / glad</u> to see his family.

d. His brother and his sister always watch <u>baseball games / relatives</u>.

e. They have different <u>opinions / reunions</u> about the game.

f. There's a red <u>balloon / banner</u> in the living room.

g. The adults <u>laugh / misbehave</u>.

h. The children <u>misbehave / eat</u>.

i. It's a good <u>balloon / family</u> reunion.

4. What about you? Answer the questions.

Do you like family reunions? Do the children in your family often misbehave?

The Home

1. Check (✓) the things you have at home. Look in your dictionary for help.

Word List: The Home

☐ yard	☐ kitchen	☐ baby's room
☐ roof	☐ floor	☐ window
☐ bedroom	☐ dining area	☐ living room
☐ door	☐ attic	☐ basement
☐ bathroom	☐ kids' bedroom	☐ garage

2. Cross out the word that doesn't belong.

a. kitchen   living room   ~~window~~

b. basement   attic   yard

c. yard   kids' bedroom   baby's room

d. door   garage   window

e. floor   roof   bathroom

f. garage   dining area   kitchen

3. Look at the picture. Circle the correct words.

a. There's a big window in the basement / living room.

b. The window / door is red.

c. The roof / floor is black.

d. The garage has two doors / floors.

e. There are five floors / windows.

f. The basement / attic has two windows.

4. Label the apartment. Write the numbers.

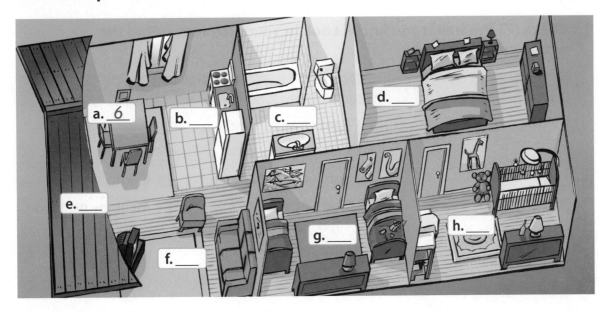

a. _6_   b. ___   c. ___   d. ___   e. ___   f. ___   g. ___   h. ___

1. kids' bedroom
2. living room
3. baby's room

4. bathroom
5. kitchen
6. ~~dining area~~

7. bedroom
8. roof

5. Study the graph. Mark the sentences *T* (true) or *F* (false).

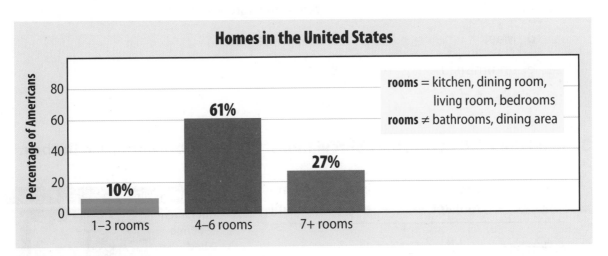

Homes in the United States

rooms = kitchen, dining room, living room, bedrooms
rooms ≠ bathrooms, dining area

Percentage of Americans

80
60
40
20
0

10%   61%   27%

1–3 rooms   4–6 rooms   7+ rooms

Based on information from: U.S. Census

a. Homes with five rooms are popular in the U.S.   _T_

b. Fifty percent of homes have three rooms.   ___

c. Ten percent of homes have 1–3 rooms.   ___

d. Seventy-one percent of homes have 1–6 rooms.   ___

CHALLENGE   How many rooms are in your home? Name the rooms.

Finding a Home

1. **Check (✓) the words you know. Look in your dictionary. Find the words you don't know.**

Word List: Finding a Home

☐ apartment search tool   ☐ **Rent** an apartment.   ☐ **Pack.**

☐ listing / classified ad   ☐ **Call** the manager.   ☐ **Unpack.**

☐ furnished apartment   ☐ **Submit** an application.   ☐ **Paint.**

☐ unfurnished apartment   ☐ **Sign** the rental agreement.   ☐ **Meet** the neighbors.

☐ utilities   ☐ **Move in.**

2. **Match the words.**

_5_ **a.** Paint   **1.** search tool

___ **b.** Submit   **2.** the neighbors.

___ **c.** Sign   **3.** the rental agreement.

___ **d.** Meet   **4.** an application.

___ **e.** unfurnished   **5.** ~~the kitchen.~~

___ **f.** apartment   **6.** apartment

3. **Read the words. Write the abbreviations. Use the abbreviations in the box.**

AC	bed	incl	mo
ba	furn apt	~~kit~~	util

a. kitchen _____kit_____

b. furnished apartment _____

c. bathroom _____

d. utilities _____

e. included _____

f. air conditioning _____

g. bedroom _____

h. month _____

Apartment Rentals ▾

Apt for rent
$900/mo
2 bed
1 ba
furn apt
util incl

✉ **Contact Property**

Apt for rent
$1100/mo
3 bed
2 ba
AC

✉ **Contact Property**

4. Look at the pictures. Put the sentences in order (1–8).

___ Move in.

___ Sign the rental agreement.

_1_ Look at classified ads.

___ Pack.

___ Submit an application.

___ Find the right apartment.

___ Call the manager.

___ Unpack.

5. Complete the crossword puzzle.

ACROSS

1. ___ an application.

3. ___ the boxes.

5. ___ an apartment.

6. Use an apartment search ___.

7. ___ the neighbors.

DOWN

1. ___ the rental agreement.

2. Find the right ___ .

3. Pay for the ___ .

4. ___ the manager.

				¹S	U	B	M	I	T
²									
			³				⁴		
⁵									
			⁶						
		⁷							

Apartments

1. Check (✓) the people and things you see every day. Look in your dictionary for help.

Word List: Apartments
☐ apartment building   ☐ parking space   ☐ prospective tenant
☐ elevator   ☐ trash bin   ☐ smoke detector
☐ stairs   ☐ emergency exit   ☐ key
☐ mailboxes   ☐ landlord
☐ security gate   ☐ lease

2. Cross out the word that doesn't belong.

a. mailbox   key   ~~emergency exit~~

b. elevator   apartment building   stairs

c. security gate   parking space   landlord

d. lease   smoke detector   emergency exit

e. landlord   prospective tenant   trash bin

3. Look at the picture. Complete the sentences. Use the Word List for help.

a. Mr. Ramos is the _____*landlord*_____.

b. The prospective tenant is signing a _____.

c. Mr. Ramos has the _____.

d. A woman is in the _____.

e. The _____ detector is above the _____.

f. There's a boy on the _____.

4. Look at the pictures. Check (✓) the correct sentences.

a. [✓] The apartment building is on Main Street.

[ ] The security gate is on Main Street.

b. [ ] The security gate is open.

[ ] The elevator door is open.

c. [ ] There are six smoke detectors.

[ ] There are six mailboxes and a smoke detector.

d. [ ] The trash bin is next to the parking space.

[ ] The trash bin is next to the park.

e. [ ] The building is for one year.

[ ] The lease is for one year.

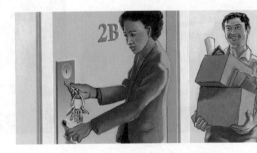

f. [ ] The landlord has the key.

[ ] The landlord has the smoke detector.

5. What about you? Answer the questions. Write *Yes, it does* or *No, it doesn't*.

a. Does your home have a smoke detector? _____.

b. Does your home have parking spaces? _____.

c. Does your home have stairs? _____.

d. Does your home have a security gate? _____.

Different Places to Live

1. Check (✓) the places you would like to live. Look in your dictionary for help.

Word List: Different Places to Live		
☐ the city	☐ the country	☐ mobile home
☐ the suburbs	☐ condo	☐ senior housing
☐ a small town	☐ townhouse	

2. Match to complete the sentences.

_5_ **a.** Tan likes his condo because . . .

___ **b.** We like senior housing because . . .

___ **c.** Jack likes the city because . . .

___ **d.** Ann likes the country because . . .

___ **e.** They like the suburbs because . . .

1. . . . they're near the city.

2. . . . there aren't many houses there.

3. . . . it's busy every minute of the day.

4. . . . we can talk to other seniors.

5. . . . ~~it has two parking spaces~~.

3. Look at the pictures. Circle the correct words.

a. It's a (mobile home)/ townhouse.

b. It's night in the small town / city.

c. They like their home in the suburbs / country.

d. Rayville is a big city / small town.

e. Kristy's townhouse / mobile home is in the city.

f. This senior housing / suburb is very popular.

1. **Check (✓) the things you see outside every day. Look in your dictionary for help.**

Word List: A House and Yard
☐ mailbox ☐ patio ☐ sprinkler
☐ driveway ☐ flower bed ☐ garbage can
☐ front door ☐ hose ☐ lawn

2. **Complete the words. Write the letters.**

a. d _r_ i _v_ e w _a_ y

b. p a t ___ ___

c. ___ o s ___

d. l ___ ___ n

e. m ___ ___ lb ___ ___

f. f l ___ ___ ___ r ___ e ___

3. **Label the picture. Use the words in the box.**

flower bed ~~front door~~ garbage can hose lawn sprinkler

a. *front door*

b. _____

c. _____

d. _____

e. _____

f. _____

CHALLENGE   Which word from the Word List is NOT in the picture?

A Kitchen

1. Check (✓) the things you use every week. Look in your dictionary for help.

Word List: A Kitchen		
☐ sink	☐ freezer	☐ stove
☐ dishwasher	☐ microwave	☐ oven
☐ refrigerator	☐ pot	☐ pan

2. Cross out the word that doesn't belong.

a. sink   dishwasher   ~~microwave~~

b. oven   stove   refrigerator

c. freezer   oven   refrigerator

d. pan   pot   freezer

e. sink   oven   microwave

3. What's wrong with the picture? Circle the correct words.

a. The (refrigerator) / freezer door is open.

b. The oven / dishwasher doesn't have a door.

c. The stove / microwave is too hot.

d. There's too much water in the dishwasher / sink.

e. The pot / pan is on the floor.

f. The pot / pan is too hot.

1. **Check (✓) the things you use every morning. Look in your dictionary for help.**

Word List: A Dining Area		
☐ plate	☐ knife	☐ dining room chair
☐ bowl	☐ spoon	☐ dining room table
☐ fork	☐ coffee mug	☐ napkin

2. **What do they need? Match the words with the pictures.**

_2_ **a.** coffee mug

___ **b.** napkin

___ **c.** plate

___ **d.** knife and fork

___ **e.** table

___ **f.** spoon

1.

2.

3.

4.

5.

6.

3. **Label the picture. Write the numbers.**

1. ~~fork~~

2. chair

3. knife

4. plate

5. spoon

6. table

7. napkin

b. ___ c. ___ e. ___ d. ___ a. _1_ g. ___ f. ___

CHALLENGE   Which two things from the Word List are NOT in the picture?

1. **Check (✓) the things people turn on and off. Look in your dictionary for help.**

Word List: A Living Room

☐ TV   ☐ fireplace   ☐ coffee table

☐ digital video recorder (DVR)   ☐ floor lamp   ☐ armchair

☐ stereo system   ☐ sofa   ☐ carpet

2. **Unscramble the words.**

    a. fosa   s <u>o</u> f <u>a</u>

    b. cerpat   c a __ p __ __

    c. amrchiar   __ r m __ h __ __ r

    d. ficreplae   f __ __ __ p l __ __ __

    e. roofl lapm   f l __ __ __ __   l __ __ p

    f. feecof atble   c __ f f __ __   t __ b __ __

3. **Read the sentences. Complete the picture.**

    a. ~~Draw a stereo system on the table next to the sofa.~~

    b. Draw an armchair next to the fireplace.

    c. Draw a TV above the DVR.

    d. Draw a floor lamp next to the sofa.

    e. Draw a coffee table in front of the sofa.

1. Check (✓) the things that use water. Look in your dictionary for help.

Word List: A Bathroom		
☐ bathtub	☐ shower curtain	☐ toilet paper
☐ soap	☐ towel	☐ toilet
☐ showerhead	☐ mirror	☐ sink

2. Complete the words. Write the letters.

a. s h _o_ w _e_ r _h e a d_

b. __ i __ k

c. m i __ __ o r

d. s __ __ p

e. __ o __ l __ t

f. __ o __ __ l

g. b __ t __ t __ __

h. t __ __ l __ t p __ p __ __

3. Label the pictures. Write the numbers.

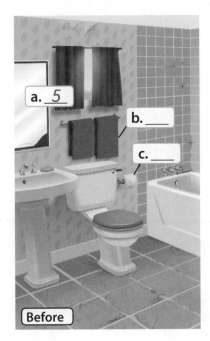

a. _5_
b. ___
c. ___

Before

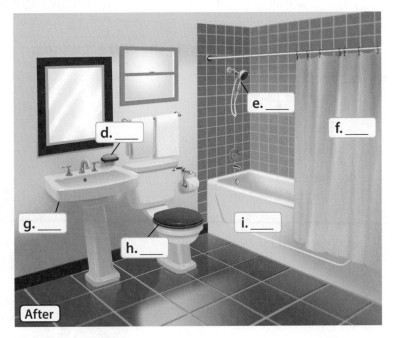

e. ___
f. ___
d. ___
g. ___
h. ___
i. ___

After

1. toilet
2. towels
3. shower curtain
4. bathtub
5. ~~mirror~~
6. soap
7. showerhead
8. sink
9. toilet paper

CHALLENGE Name the things in the "after" picture that are new.

1. **Check (✓) the things in your bedroom. Look in your dictionary for help.**

Word List: A Bedroom

☐ dresser   ☐ bed   ☐ blanket

☐ closet   ☐ pillow   ☐ night table

☐ curtains   ☐ sheet   ☐ lamp

2. **Look at the picture in Exercise 3. Match the words with the sentences.**

_2_ **a.** clothes   **1.** They're on the window.

___ **b.** sheets   **2.** ~~They're in the dresser and on the floor.~~

___ **c.** curtains   **3.** It's on the bed.

___ **d.** lamp   **4.** It's next to the bed.

___ **e.** night table   **5.** They're on the bed.

___ **f.** pillow   **6.** It's on the night table.

3. **Look at the picture. Circle the correct words.**

a. The (blanket)/ pillow is on the floor.

b. There's a towel on the night table / bed.

c. There's a phone and a lamp / sheet on the night table.

d. The night table / closet is open.

e. There are some clothes on the dresser / blanket.

f. The night table / curtains are pink.

g. The girl is in the bed / closet.

h. There are books under the bed / pillow.

1. Check (✓) the kids' bedroom furniture. Look in your dictionary for help.

Word List: The Kids' Bedroom		
☐ changing table	☐ baby monitor	☐ toy chest
☐ crib	☐ bunk beds	☐ blocks
☐ chest of drawers	☐ ball	☐ doll

2. Cross out the word that doesn't belong.

a. ~~toy chest~~   bunk beds   crib

b. crib   kids' bedroom   changing table

c. blocks   changing table   ball

d. toy chest   baby monitor   chest of drawers

e. ball   doll   bunk beds

3. Read the sentences. Complete the picture.

a. ~~Draw a doll on the changing table.~~

b. Draw a baby monitor on the chest of drawers.

c. Draw a toy chest next to the crib.

d. Draw some blocks on the bunk beds.

e. Draw a ball on the toy chest.

f. Draw a toy on the chest of drawers.

59

Housework

1. **Check (✓) the things you do every week. Look in your dictionary for help.**

<table>
<tr><td colspan="3">Word List: Housework</td></tr>
<tr><td>☐ dust the furniture</td><td>☐ make the bed</td><td>☐ sweep the floor</td></tr>
<tr><td>☐ clean the oven</td><td>☐ vacuum the carpet</td><td>☐ wash the dishes</td></tr>
<tr><td>☐ mop the floor</td><td>☐ wash the windows</td><td>☐ take out the garbage</td></tr>
</table>

2. **Match the words.**

_4_ **a.** wash   **1.** the furniture

___ **b.** make   **2.** the garbage

___ **c.** dust   **3.** the carpet

___ **d.** mop   **4.** the windows

___ **e.** vacuum   **5.** the floor

___ **f.** take out   **6.** the bed

3. **Look at the picture. Read the sentences. Number the people.**

1. Jim vacuums the carpet.   **3.** Paul takes out the garbage.   **5.** Lian sweeps the floor.

2. Wen washes the windows.   **4.** Mira cleans the oven.   **6.** Hua washes the dishes.

1. Check (✓) the things you have at home. Look in your dictionary for help.

Word List: Cleaning Supplies

☐ rubber gloves   ☐ cleaning cloths   ☐ broom

☐ mop   ☐ vacuum cleaner   ☐ dish towel

☐ bucket   ☐ glass cleaner   ☐ trash bags

2. Match the sentences with the words.

_6_ **a.** I have to clean the oven.

___ **b.** I have to mop the floor.

___ **c.** She wants to sweep the floor.

___ **d.** Please help me with the dishes.

___ **e.** They want to wash the windows.

___ **f.** He's taking out the garbage.

___ **g.** I want to vacuum the carpet.

1. vacuum cleaner

2. broom

3. glass cleaner and cleaning cloths

4. trash bag

5. dish towel

6. ~~rubber gloves and cleaning cloths~~

7. bucket and a mop

3. Label the cleaning supplies. Write the numbers.

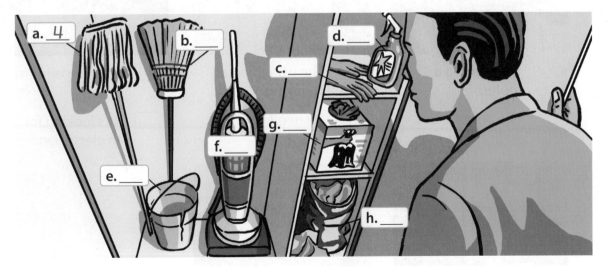

a. 4   b. ___   c. ___   d. ___   e. ___   f. ___   g. ___   h. ___

1. broom   **3.** glass cleaner   **5.** cleaning cloths   **7.** trash bags

2. bucket   **4.** ~~mop~~   **6.** rubber gloves   **8.** vacuum

CHALLENGE   Look at the picture. What does Sam need to buy?

Household Problems and Repairs

1. Check (✓) the problems you can fix. Look in your dictionary for help.

Word List: Household Problems and Repairs

☐ The water heater is **not working**.　☐ The window is **broken**.　☐ electrician

☐ The power is **out**.　☐ The lock is **broken**.　☐ repairperson

☐ The roof is **leaking**.　☐ roofer　☐ locksmith

2. Unscramble the sentences.

a. The broken. is lock　　　　*The lock is broken.*

b. is power The out.　　　　_____

c. roof The leaking. is　　　　_____

d. broken. is window The　　　　_____

e. heater isn't The water working.　_____

3. Look at the pictures. Check (✓) the correct sentences.

a. ☑ She's calling a roofer.

☐ The power is out.

b. ☐ The water heater is leaking.

☐ He needs a locksmith.

c. ☐ He's a repairperson.

☐ He's looking for an electrician.

d. ☐ He needs an electrician.

☐ He needs a locksmith.

e. ☐ The window is broken.

☐ She's a repairperson.

4. Check (✓) the problems you sometimes have at home.

Word List: Household Problems and Repairs
☐ The pipes are **frozen.** ☐ plumber ☐ cockroaches
☐ The sink is **overflowing.** ☐ exterminator ☐ rats
☐ The toilet is **stopped up.** ☐ termites ☐ mice

5. Complete the chart. Use all the words in the Word List.

People	Plumbing Problems	Pests
a. *plumber*	c.	f.
b.	d.	g.
	e.	h.
		i.

6. Study the chart. Write the answers.

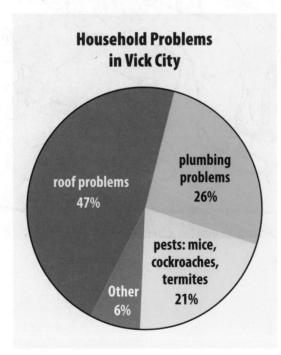

Household Problems in Vick City

roof problems 47%

plumbing problems 26%

pests: mice, cockroaches, termites 21%

Other 6%

a. What percentage of homes have plumbing problems? ___26%___

b. What is the biggest problem in Vick City? _____

c. Name three pests in Vick City.
_____
_____
_____

d. Name two or more plumbing problems.
_____
_____

e. Name one or more "other" problems.
_____

CHALLENGE Which household problems and repairs are expensive?

63

1. Check (✓) the words you know. Look in your dictionary. Find the words you don't know.

Word List: The Tenant Meeting			
☐ roommates	☐ DJ	☐ rules	☐ invitation
☐ party	☐ noise	☐ mess	☐ **dance**
☐ music	☐ irritated		

2. Look at the picture. Write *T* (true) or *F* (false).

a. The people are having a party. _F_

b. They're having a tenant meeting. ___

c. The tenants are making some rules. ___

d. A DJ is playing music. ___

e. They're irritated by loud music. ___

f. They're writing an invitation. ___

g. The room is a big mess. ___

3. Look at the pictures. Circle the correct words.

a. Marvin is having a <u>meeting</u> / (party) tonight.

b. The party is for the <u>noise / tenants</u>.

c. Chad is a <u>DJ / manager</u>.

d. He's playing <u>music / rules</u>.

e. Some of the tenants are <u>dancing / irritated</u>.

f. There's <u>a big mess / a lot of noise</u>, but everybody is happy.

4. What about you? Answer the questions. Write *Yes, I do* or *No, I don't.*

a. Do you have roommates?   _____.

b. Do you have rules about noise and music in your home?   _____.

Back from the Market

1. **Check (✓) the things you keep in the refrigerator. Look in your dictionary for help.**

Word List: Back from the Market		
☐ fish	☐ butter	☐ bread
☐ meat	☐ eggs	☐ pasta
☐ chicken	☐ vegetables	☐ grocery bag
☐ cheese	☐ fruit	☐ shopping list
☐ milk	☐ rice	☐ coupons

2. **Label the ad. Use the words in the box.**

milk   ~~coupons~~   eggs   fruit   pasta   bread

a. coupons
b. _____
c. _____
d. _____
e. _____
f. _____

3. **Read the sentences. Circle the correct words.**

a. I'm back from the market. Everything is in the (grocery bags)/ coupons.

b. You can save money with coupons / a grocery bag.

c. Please put the fish / shopping list in the refrigerator.

d. Tom doesn't eat meat / milk, but he eats eggs and fish.

66

4. Label the pictures. Use the words in the box.

bread	cheese	eggs	fish	fruit
meat	~~milk~~	pasta	vegetables	

a. __milk__   b. _____   c. _____   d. _____   e. _____

f. _____   g. _____   h. _____   i. _____

5. Look at the picture. Complete the shopping list.

Mmm, Mmm, good for dinner tonight!

Shopping List

a. _r_ ic _e_

b. chi___k___n

c. v___g___t___bles

d. b___ ___t___r

e. ch___ ___s___

CHALLENGE   List the food you eat every day.

Fruit

1. **Check (✓) the fruit you like to eat. Look in your dictionary for help.**

Word List: Fruit		
☐ apples	☐ pears	☐ peaches
☐ bananas	☐ oranges	☐ strawberries
☐ grapes	☐ lemons	☐ melons

2. **Unscramble the words.**

   a. cepeash   _p_ e _a_ c h _e_ _s_

   b. reasp   p __ __ r __

   c. paspel   __ p __ l e __

   d. gorenas   __ __ a __ __ e s

   e. prages   __ __ a __ e __

   f. naaansb   b __ __ a __ __ s

3. **Label the picture. Write the numbers.**

a. _8_
b. ___
c. ___
d. ___
e. ___
f. ___
g. ___
h. ___
i. ___

1. bananas	4. peaches	7. pears
2. strawberries	5. grapes	8. ~~apples~~
3. lemons	6. melons	9. oranges

1. Check (✓) the things you eat every week. Look in your dictionary for help.

Word List: Vegetables

☐ lettuce   ☐ bell peppers   ☐ potatoes

☐ carrots   ☐ celery   ☐ onions

☐ tomatoes   ☐ corn   ☐ mushrooms

2. Look at the picture. Circle the vegetables. Then write the answers.

a. How many bell peppers are there? _3_

b. How many tomatoes are there? ___

c. How many onions are there? ___

d. How many potatoes are there? ___

3. Look at the pictures. Write the recipes.

a. **Four Veggie Juice**

1 _____

5 _____

4 _____

3 _____

b. **Hot Days Juice**

1 cup _lettuce_

1 _____

1 red _____

1/2 cabbage

c. **Sweet Dreams Juice**

3 _____

4 _____

2 stalks _____

1 cup _____

CHALLENGE Circle the juice you want to try.

Meat and Poultry

1. Check (✓) the things in your refrigerator now. Look in your dictionary for help.

Word List: Meat and Poultry

Beef	Pork	Lamb	Poultry
☐ roast	☐ ham	☐ lamb chops	☐ chicken
☐ steak	☐ bacon		☐ turkey
☐ ground beef	☐ sausage		

2. Complete the menu. Use the words in the box.

meat   ~~steak~~   ham   bacon   sausage   lamb chops   chicken   turkey

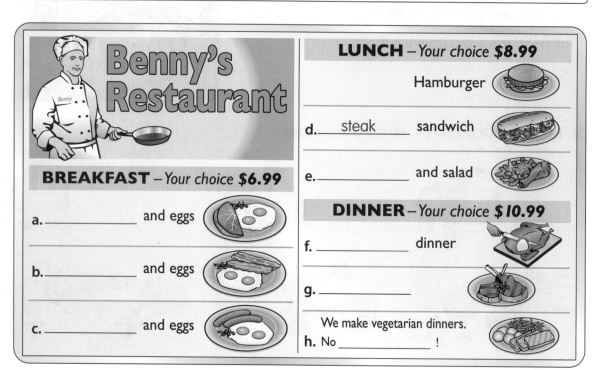

Benny's Restaurant

BREAKFAST – *Your choice* **$6.99**

a. _____ and eggs

b. _____ and eggs

c. _____ and eggs

LUNCH – *Your choice* **$8.99**

Hamburger

d. ___steak___ sandwich

e. _____ and salad

DINNER – *Your choice* **$10.99**

f. _____ dinner

g. _____

We make vegetarian dinners.
h. No _____ !

3. Use the menu in Exercise 2. Answer the questions. Write *yes* or *no*.

a. Is there pork on the menu?   ___yes___

b. Is there ground beef on the menu?   _____

c. Is there roast on the menu?   _____

d. Is there poultry on the menu?   _____

e. Is there fruit on the menu?   _____

1. Check (✓) the things you like to eat. Look in your dictionary for help.

Word List: Seafood and Deli

☐ salmon   ☐ wheat bread   ☐ American cheese

☐ shrimp   ☐ roast beef   ☐ Swiss cheese

☐ frozen fish   ☐ smoked turkey   ☐ cheddar cheese

2. Complete the chart. Use the words in the box.

roast beef   shrimp   American cheese   ~~frozen fish~~   cheddar cheese   smoked turkey

 Seafood	 Meat	Cheese
a. *frozen fish*	c.	e.
b.	d.	f.

3. Look at the pictures. Circle the correct words.

a. Rebecca likes cheddar cheese / (roast beef.)

b. Armando likes Swiss cheese / cheddar cheese.

c. Sam likes smoked turkey/ Swiss cheese.

d. Wilma likes American cheese / wheat bread.

e. Su Ling likes salmon / shrimp.

f. Charlie likes frozen fish / cheddar cheese.

A Grocery Store

1. Check (✓) the things you often buy at a grocery store. Look in your dictionary for help.

> ### Word List: A Grocery Store
>
> | | | |
> |---|---|---|
> | ☐ customer | **Canned Foods** | **Baking Products** |
> | ☐ aisle | ☐ beans | ☐ flour |
> | ☐ manager | ☐ tuna | ☐ sugar |
> | ☐ line | **Dairy** | ☐ oil |
> | ☐ cart | ☐ yogurt | **Baked Goods** |
> | ☐ cashier | **Frozen Foods** | ☐ cookies |
> | ☐ bagger | ☐ ice cream | ☐ cake |

2. Cross out the word that doesn't belong.

a. customer ~~ice cream~~ bagger **d.** ice cream cake tuna

b. manager line aisle **e.** beans flour sugar

c. tuna beans cashier **f.** yogurt flour ice cream

3. Label the pictures. Use the words in the box.

yogurt	bagger	cookies	~~customer~~	manager	tuna

a. _____customer_____

b. _____

c. _____

d. _____

e. _____

f. _____

4. Look at the picture. Write *T* (true) or *F* (false).

a. There are three customers.   _T_   e. He's also buying cake.   ___

b. The cashier is happy.   ___   f. Two women are in line.   ___

c. Two customers have carts.   ___   g. The bagger is happy.   ___

d. The man is buying a bottle of oil.   ___   h. The women are buying ice cream.   ___

5. Look at the store directory. Answer the questions.

a. Where can you find canned beans?   _aisle 2_

b. Where can you find cookies?   _____

c. Where can you find yogurt?   _____

d. Where can you find sugar?   _____

e. Where can you find turkey and cheese?   _____

f. Where can you find ice cream?   _____

g. Where can you find milk?   _____

h. Where can you find vegetables?   _____

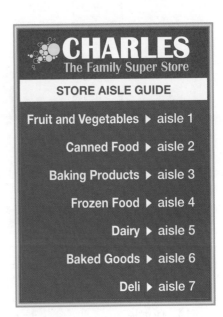

CHARLES
The Family Super Store

STORE AISLE GUIDE

Fruit and Vegetables ▶ aisle 1

Canned Food ▶ aisle 2

Baking Products ▶ aisle 3

Frozen Food ▶ aisle 4

Dairy ▶ aisle 5

Baked Goods ▶ aisle 6

Deli ▶ aisle 7

CHALLENGE   Name two places in the grocery store where the food is cold.

Containers and Packaging

1. **Check (✓) the things you have in the refrigerator. Look in your dictionary for help.**

Word List: Containers and Packaging		
☐ bottle	☐ carton	☐ bag
☐ jar	☐ container	☐ six-pack
☐ can	☐ box	☐ loaf

2. **Complete the words. Write the letters.**

   a. j a _r_

   b. ___ ___ x

   c. ___ ___ g

   d. ___ ___ n

   e. b ___ ___ t l ___

   f. c ___ n ___ a ___ n ___ ___

   g. c ___ r ___ ___ n

   h. l ___ ___ f

3. **Label the picture. Write the numbers.**

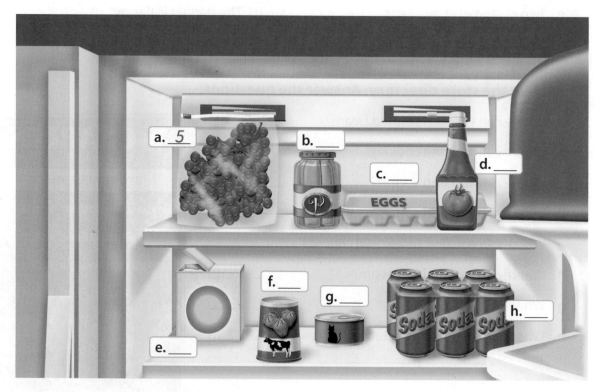

1. bottle	3. container	5. ~~bag~~	7. jar
2. can	4. box	6. carton	8. six-pack

1. **Check (✓) the words you know. Look in your dictionary. Find the words you don't know.**

Word List: Weights and Measurements		
☐ a cup of oil	☐ a gallon of water	☐ a cup of flour
☐ a pint of yogurt	☐ a teaspoon of salt	☐ an ounce of cheese
☐ a quart of milk	☐ a tablespoon of sugar	☐ a pound of roast beef

2. **Read the words. Write the abbreviations. Use the abbreviations in the box.**

qt.	pt.	~~c.~~	lb.	tsp.	oz.	gal.	TBS.

a. cup __c.__ **c.** pint _____ **e.** teaspoon _____ **g.** ounce _____

b. quart _____ **d.** gallon _____ **f.** tablespoon _____ **h.** pound _____

3. **Which is more? Write the answers.**

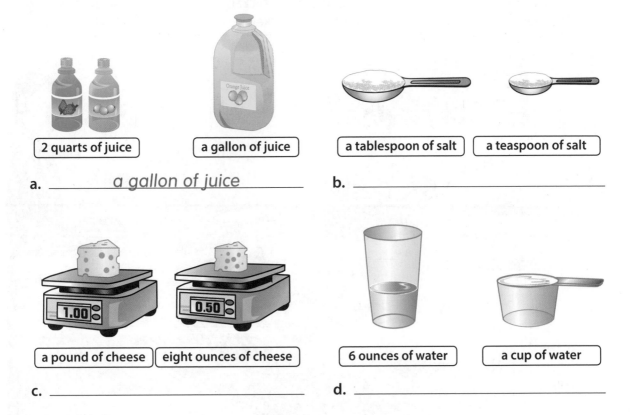

2 quarts of juice | a gallon of juice   a tablespoon of salt | a teaspoon of salt

a. _a gallon of juice_ **b.** _____

a pound of cheese | eight ounces of cheese   6 ounces of water | a cup of water

c. _____ **d.** _____

CHALLENGE How many quarts are in a gallon? How many ounces are in a pound?

Food Preparation and Safety

1. Check (✓) the words you know. Look in your dictionary. Find the words you don't know.

Word List: Food Preparation and Safety		
☐ clean	☐ fried	☐ boiled
☐ cook	☐ barbecued	☐ stir-fried
☐ chill	☐ roasted	☐ scrambled

2. Unscramble the words.

a. bolied <u>b</u> o <u>i</u> l e <u>d</u>

b. steorad r __ __ a s __ __ d

c. diref __ __ r i __ __

d. ilhlc __ __ __ __ l

e. ancle __ __ __ e a __

f. okoc c __ __ __ __

3. Label the picture. Use the words in the box.

fried chicken	~~barbecued chicken~~	scrambled eggs
stir-fried vegetables	roasted chicken	boiled eggs

a. _____

b. _____

c. _____

d. _barbecued chicken_

e. _____

f. _____

4. Check (✓) the things you do to prepare your favorite food. Look in your dictionary for help.

Word List: Food Preparation and Safety		
☐ preheat	☐ bake	☐ chop
☐ slice	☐ cut up	☐ boil
☐ steam	☐ peel	☐ mix

5. How do you prepare these foods? Check (✓) the correct words.

a.	b.	c.	d.
☐ mix	☐ boil	☐ chop	☐ steam
✓ peel	☐ slice	☐ bake	☐ preheat

6. Look at the pictures. Complete the recipe. Use the words in the box.

Mix	Slice	Peel	~~Preheat~~	Cut up	Chop

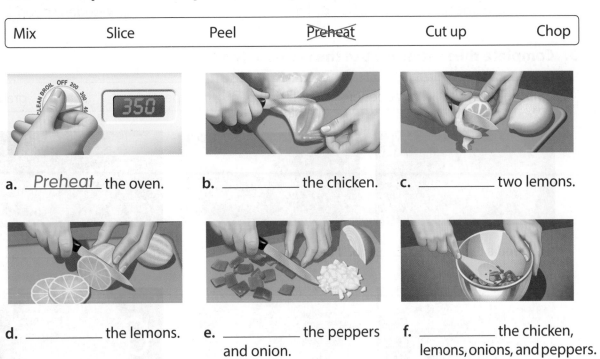

a. _Preheat_ the oven.

b. _____ the chicken.

c. _____ two lemons.

d. _____ the lemons.

e. _____ the peppers and onion.

f. _____ the chicken, lemons, onions, and peppers.

Kitchen Utensils

1. Check (✓) the things you have in your kitchen. Look in your dictionary for help.

Word List: Kitchen Utensils		
☐ can opener	☐ frying pan	☐ vegetable peeler
☐ grater	☐ pot	☐ lid
☐ steamer	☐ wooden spoon	☐ mixing bowl

2. Match the words with the pictures.

1.
2.
3.

4.
5.
6.

_4_ **a.** steamer   ___ **c.** frying pan   ___ **e.** pot

___ **b.** can opener   ___ **d.** lid   ___ **f.** wooden spoon

3. Complete the sentences. Use the words in the box.

mixing bowl   can opener   ~~frying pan~~   peeler   lid   grater

a. I need a _frying pan_ .   **b.** I need a _____.   **c.** I need a _____.

  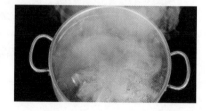

d. I need a _____.   **e.** I need a _____.   **f.** I need a _____.

78

1. **Check (✓) your three favorite fast foods. Look in your dictionary for help.**

Word List: A Fast Food Restaurant		
☐ hamburger	☐ hot dog	☐ pizza
☐ French fries	☐ nachos	☐ soda
☐ cheeseburger	☐ taco	☐ donut

2. **Complete the menu. Use the words in the box.**

hot dog   ~~nachos~~   taco   soda   pizza   donuts

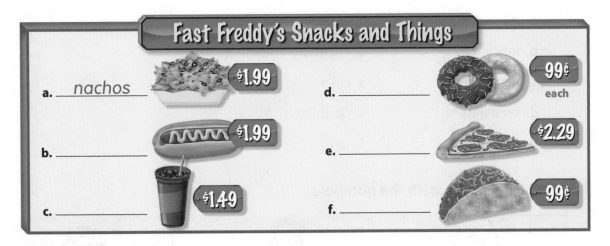

Fast Freddy's Snacks and Things

a. _nachos_ $1.99

b. _____ $1.99

c. _____ $1.49

d. _____ 99¢ each

e. _____ $2.29

f. _____ 99¢

3. **Study the graph. Answer the questions.**

a. What is the favorite fast food for girls? _French fries_

b. What is the favorite fast food for boys? _____

c. Which food is the same for boys and girls? _____

d. Look at the Word List. Name an example of "other" fast food. _____

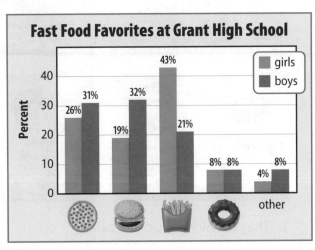

Fast Food Favorites at Grant High School

girls
boys

26% 31% 19% 32% 43% 21% 8% 8% 4% 8%

other

CHALLENGE Look at the menu in Exercise 2. Write your order and the total price.

A Coffee Shop Menu

1. Check (✓) the things you like to eat and drink. Look in your dictionary for help.

Word List: A Coffee Shop Menu			
Breakfast	**Lunch**	**Dinner**	**Dessert**
☐ toast	☐ sandwich	☐ spaghetti	☐ cake
☐ pancakes	☐ salad	☐ meatballs	☐ pie
☐ cereal	☐ soup	☐ grilled fish	**Beverages**
		☐ meatloaf	☐ coffee
			☐ tea

2. Match the words.

_2_ **a.** dinner

___ **b.** lunch

___ **c.** beverage

___ **d.** breakfast

___ **e.** dessert

1. soup and a sandwich

2. ~~spaghetti and meatballs~~

3. cake

4. pancakes

5. tea

3. Label the picture with the numbers.

a. _4_

b. ___

c. ___

d. ___

e. ___

f. ___

1. They're having soup and salad.

2. They're having meatloaf and vegetables.

3. She's having cereal and tea.

4. ~~She's having coffee and toast.~~

5. They're having sandwiches.

6. She's having pancakes and eggs.

4. Look at the picture. Complete the guest check. Then answer the questions.

	Guest Check				223458
DATE	TABLE	GUESTS	SERVER		

APPT-SOUP/SAL-ENTREE-VEG/POT-DESSERT-BEV

	g r i l l e d f i sh	$9.99
	s __ ag __ et ____ and	
	m __ at __ a __ __ s	$7.99
	c __ k __	$3.99
	p __ __	$3.99
2	c __ f f __ __ s	$1.98
		TAX
		TOTAL

THANK YOU - PLEASE COME AGAIN.

a. How much is dessert? _____$7.98_____

b. How much are the beverages? _____

c. Which item is $9.99? _____

d. Is this breakfast, lunch, or dinner? _____

5. What about you? Answer the questions.

a. What is the name of your favorite restaurant? _____

b. Is that restaurant a coffee shop or a fast food restaurant? _____

c. What do you usually order there? _____

d. Do you usually go there for breakfast, lunch, or dinner? _____

81

1. **Check (✓) the words you know. Look in your dictionary. Find the words you don't know.**

Word List: A Restaurant		
☐ hostess	☐ **set** the table	☐ **pay** the check
☐ high chair	☐ **seat** the customer	☐ **leave** a tip
☐ booth	☐ **order** from the menu	
☐ menu	☐ **take** the order	
☐ server	☐ **serve** the meal	
☐ busser	☐ **clear** the dishes	

2. **Complete the chart. Use the words in the box.**

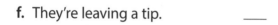

menu   serve   table   pay   order   clear   dishes

Customer	Server	Busser
a. order from the _menu_	**c.** take the _____	**e.** set the _____
b. _____ the check	**d.** _____ the meal	**f.** _____ the _____

3. **Look at the picture. Write *T* (true) or *F* (false).**

a. The menus are on the table.   _T_

b. The server is at the table.   ___

c. There's a high chair at the table. ___

d. They want to pay the check. ___

e. They want to order now. ___

f. They're leaving a tip. ___

4. Read the sentences. Label the picture with the numbers.

1. Carmen is a customer. She needs a high chair for the baby.

2. Lee is a server. He's taking an order.

3. ~~Joe is a busser. He's setting a table.~~

4. Al is sitting in a booth with his friend.

5. Nora is a hostess. She's seating a customer.

6. Iris is a busser. She's clearing a table.

7. Pablo is paying the check.

8. Ina is a server. She's serving a meal.

5. Read the ads. Circle the correct words.

HELP WANTED
at family restaurant.
Take orders, serve food. Must learn menu. Free lunch, good tips.
555-3254 days.

RESTAURANT HELP
WANTED
Set tables and clear dishes, clean booths. Some tips, good hours. **314 Main St.**

a. This job is for a <u>hostess</u> / (<u>server</u>).

b. At this restaurant the customers leave good <u>lunch</u> / <u>tips</u>.

c. You need to study the <u>menu</u> / <u>server</u> for this job.

d. This job is for a <u>busser</u> / <u>hostess</u>.

e. You need to clear <u>high chair</u> / <u>dishes</u> and clean <u>orders</u> / <u>booths</u> at this job.

f. You get some <u>lunch</u> / <u>tips</u> at this job.

The Farmers' Market

1. **Check (✓) the words you know. Look in your dictionary. Find the words you don't know.**

<table>
<tr><td colspan="4">Word List: The Farmers' Market</td></tr>
<tr><td>☐ live music</td><td>☐ sour</td><td>☐ vendors</td><td>☐ herbs</td></tr>
<tr><td>☐ organic</td><td>☐ samples</td><td>☐ sweets</td><td>☐ count</td></tr>
<tr><td>☐ lemonade</td><td>☐ avocados</td><td></td><td></td></tr>
</table>

2. **Match the words with the pictures.**

_1_ **a.** sweets

___ **b.** organic herbs

___ **c.** sour lemonade

___ **d.** live music

___ **e.** vendor

___ **f.** avocados

___ **g.** count

___ **h.** samples

3. Look at the pictures. Circle the correct words.

a. We go to the (farmers) / sweet market every Sunday.

b. I like the <u>live / sour</u> music.

c. My son likes the free <u>samples / vendors</u>.

d. We buy <u>organic / sour</u> vegetables there.

e. Sometimes we <u>buy herbs / count vendors</u>.

f. Today we are buying <u>samples / avocados</u>.

g. My son is drinking <u>lemonade / avocados</u>. It's sweet.

h. I'm <u>counting / buying</u> my money.

4. What about you? Answer the questions. Write _Yes, there is_ or _No, there isn't._

a. Is there a farmers' market near your home? _____

b. Is there a place to buy organic food near your home? _____

c. Is there a place to listen to live music near your home? _____

Everyday Clothes

1. **Check (✓) the clothes you wear often. Look in your dictionary for help.**

Word List: Everyday Clothes			
☐ shirt	☐ baseball cap	☐ handbag	☐ shoes
☐ jeans	☐ socks	☐ skirt	☐ sweater
☐ dress	☐ sneakers	☐ suit	☐ **tie**
☐ T-shirt	☐ blouse	☐ pants	☐ **put on**

2. **Cross out the word that doesn't belong.**

a. shirt	~~socks~~	blouse
b. sweater	shoes	sneakers
c. pants	jeans	shirt
d. skirt	baseball cap	dress
e. suit	T-shirt	dress
f. tie shoes	put on socks	handbag

3. **Look at the ad. Complete the sentences. Use the words in the box.**

T-shirts	sweaters	blouses	handbags	pants	~~shirts~~

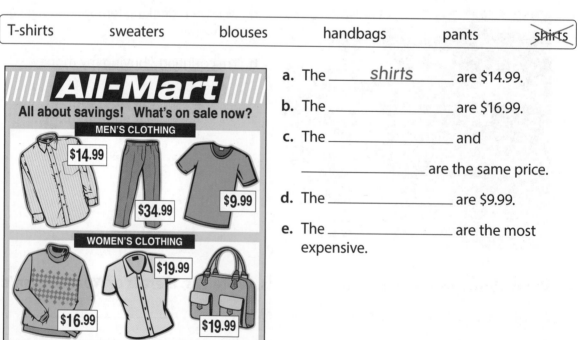

a. The _____ *shirts* _____ are $14.99.

b. The _____ are $16.99.

c. The _____ and

_____ are the same price.

d. The _____ are $9.99.

e. The _____ are the most expensive.

4. Look at the pictures. Check (✓) the correct sentences.

a. ☐ He's wearing a T-shirt.

☑ He's wearing jeans.

b. ☐ She has a handbag.

☐ She's wearing pants and a shirt.

c. ☐ Three students are wearing jeans.

☐ Three students are wearing T-shirts.

d. ☐ He's putting on his socks.

☐ He can tie his shoes.

e. ☐ They're wearing socks and jeans.

☐ They're wearing sneakers and caps.

f. ☐ She's wearing a skirt and blouse.

☐ He's wearing a suit.

5. Study the chart. Answer the questions.

a. What percent of people like jeans the best? _56%_

b. What percent like dresses or suits the best? _____

c. What percent like pants and shirts the best? _____

d. What percent of people don't like jeans the best? _____

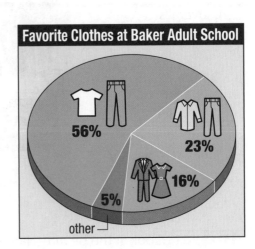

Favorite Clothes at Baker Adult School

56%

23%

16%

5%

other

Casual, Work, and Formal Clothes

1. Check (✓) the clothes you like to wear. Look in your dictionary for help.

Word List: Casual, Work, and Formal Clothes			
☐ sport shirt	☐ uniform	☐ tuxedo	☐ sweatshirt
☐ overalls	☐ business suit	☐ evening gown	☐ sweatpants
☐ knit top	☐ tie		☐ tank top
☐ sandals	☐ briefcase		☐ shorts

2. Unscramble the words.

Casual and Exercise Clothes

a. storsh   s h _o_ _r_ t s

b. slandsa   s __ n d __ __ s

c. ktan opt   __ __ __ __

                 __ __ __ __

d. torps trish   __ __ __ __ __

                 __ __ __ __ __

Formal and Work Clothes

e. otuxed   t __ x __ __ __

f. sibesuns tusi   b __ si __ e __ s s __ __ t

g. ite   __ __ __

h. enevgin wnog   __ __ __ __ __ __ __

                         __ __ __ __

3. Label the picture. Write the numbers.

1. briefcase
2. ~~business suit~~
3. knit top
4. overalls

a. _2_ b. ___ c. ___ d. ___

CHALLENGE Look at the picture. Name the shoes you see.

88

4. **Look at the picture. Read the sentences. Number the people.**

a. 2

b. ____

c. ____

d. ____

e. ____

f. ____

g. ____

1. Jack is wearing a uniform.

2. ~~Gabriel is wearing a business suit.~~

3. Ken is wearing shorts.

4. Lara is wearing overalls.

5. Grace is wearing sweatpants.

6. Anne is wearing sandals.

7. Jen is looking at a dress.

5. **What about you? Complete the sentences with *casual, work,* or *formal*.**

a. I like _____ clothes.

b. I think _____ clothes are expensive.

c. I think _____ clothes are comfortable.

d. I don't like to wear _____ clothes.

e. I usually wear _____ clothes.

Seasonal Clothing

1. Check (✓) the things you never wear or use. Look in your dictionary for help.

Word List: Seasonal Clothing

☐ hat   ☐ gloves   ☐ raincoat

☐ coat   ☐ jacket   ☐ swimsuit

☐ scarf   ☐ umbrella   ☐ sunglasses

2. Complete the chart. Use the words in the box.

gloves	raincoat	~~coat~~	sunglasses
umbrella	scarf	swimsuit	

	Cold		Rainy		Hot
a.	*coat*	**d.**		**f.**	
b.		**e.**		**g.**	
c.					

3. Look at the picture. Circle the correct words.

a. The girl is wearing a (scarf)/ hat.

b. The boy is wearing <u>a hat / sunglasses</u>.

c. The boy and the girl are wearing <u>coats / swimsuits</u>.

d. The boy and the girl are wearing <u>raincoats / gloves</u>.

e. Sam has <u>an umbrella / sunglasses</u>.

f. Sam is wearing a <u>jacket / scarf</u>.

1. Check (✓) the words you know. Look in your dictionary. Find the words you don't know.

Word List: Underwear and Sleepwear

☐ undershirt   ☐ socks   ☐ bra   ☐ nightgown

☐ boxer shorts   ☐ panties   ☐ pajamas   ☐ robe

☐ briefs   ☐ pantyhose

2. Match the words with the pictures.

1.

2.

3.

4.

5.

6.

_4_ **a.** boxer shorts   ___ **c.** socks   ___ **e.** undershirt

___ **b.** bra   ___ **d.** pantyhose   ___ **f.** briefs

3. Label the picture. Use the words in the box.

boxer shorts   ~~socks~~   pantyhose   pajamas   nightgown   robe

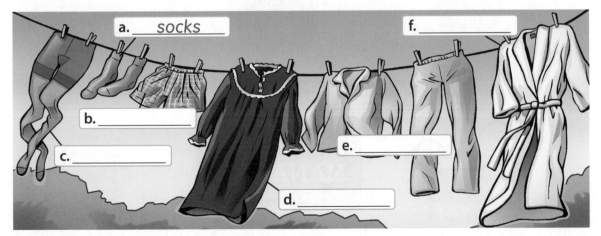

a. ___socks___

f. _____

b. _____

c. _____

e. _____

d. _____

Workplace Clothing

1. **Check (✓) the things you or your classmates wear at work. Look in your dictionary for help.**

Word List: Workplace Clothing		
☐ hard hat	☐ apron	☐ hairnet
☐ work shirt	☐ polo shirt	☐ scrubs
☐ tool belt	☐ name tag	☐ face mask
☐ coveralls	☐ work gloves	☐ lab coat
☐ safety glasses	☐ badge	☐ medical gloves

2. **Match the words.**

_5_ **a.** hard   **1.** mask

___ **b.** face   **2.** coat

___ **c.** lab   **3.** belt

___ **d.** tool   **4.** gloves

___ **e.** polo   **5.** ~~hat~~

___ **f.** medical   **6.** shirt

3. **Label the pictures. Use the words in the box.**

hairnet	apron	~~badge~~	work shirt	safety glasses	name tag

a. _____badge_____

b. _____

c. _____

d. _____

e. _____

f. _____

4. Look at the picture. Write *T* (true) or *F* (false).

a. There's a work glove on the floor. *T*

b. There's a man in coveralls. ___

c. There's a worker with safety glasses. ___

d. There's a woman in scrubs. ___

e. There's a doctor in an apron. ___

f. There are two people with gloves. ___

5. Look at the picture. Write two more things John needs to be safe.

a. ___*a hard hat*___

b. _____

c. _____

Shoes and Accessories

1. Check (✓) the shoes and accessories you have on. Look in your dictionary for help.

Word List: Shoes and Accessories

☐ purse   ☐ necklace   ☐ pumps

☐ belt   ☐ wallet   ☐ boots

☐ shoe department   ☐ watch   ☐ tennis shoes

☐ jewelry department   ☐ backpack   ☐ earrings

☐ bracelet   ☐ high heels   ☐ ring

2. Complete the chart. Use the words in the box.

backpacks	wallets	boots	earrings	tennis shoes
high heels	necklaces	purses	~~rings~~	watches
belts	pumps			

Jewelry Department	Shoe Department	Other Accessories
a. *rings*	e.	i.
b.	f.	j.
c.	g.	k.
d.	h.	l.

3. Read the sentences. Write _T_ (true) or _F_ (false).

a. You can buy earrings in the shoe department.   _F_

b. Many children use backpacks at school.   ___

c. Bracelets and pumps are in the jewelry department.   ___

d. Boots and high heels are in the shoe department.   ___

e. People keep money in their watches.   ___

f. People wear tennis shoes to exercise.   ___

4. Look at the picture. Circle the correct words.

a. The girl has a (purse) / backpack.

b. The girl is wearing a <u>watch</u> / <u>belt</u>.

c. The woman is wearing <u>boots</u> / <u>pumps</u>.

d. The girl is wearing <u>tennis shoes</u> / <u>high heels</u>.

e. There are <u>tennis shoes</u> / <u>boots</u> on the floor.

5. Look at the receipt. Complete the sentences.

```
        NICKELS
   DEPARTMENT STORE
- - - - - - - - - - - - - - - - - - - - - - - - - - -
01  MEN'S  TENNIS SHOES              $24.99
02  CHILDREN'S SHOES 2@ $10.99       $21.98
03  BOOTS                            $36.98
04  WOMEN'S ACCESSORIES: PURSE       $24.50
05  FASHION JEWELRY: RING            $12.99
06  FASHION JEWELRY: NECKLACE        $ 9.99
                         SUBTOTAL   $131.43
                              TAX    $11.50
                            TOTAL   $142.93
```

a. The ___*boots*___ cost $36.98.

b. The _____ is from the accessories department.

c. The total for jewelry is _____.

d. The total from the shoe department is _____.

CHALLENGE   Name the shoes and accessories you wear and use every day.

Describing Clothes

1. **Check (✓) the words that describe the clothes you wear. Look in your dictionary for help.**

Word List: Describing Clothes			
☐ small	☐ short-sleeved	☐ short	☐ solid
☐ medium	☐ long-sleeved	☐ long	☐ striped
☐ large			

2. **Match the words with the pictures.**

a. _2_   b. ____   c. ____   d. ____

1. large   2. ~~short~~   3. long   4. small

3. **Read the story. Put the pictures in order (1–6).**

Bita needs a new shirt. She looks at a long-sleeved blue shirt. She looks at a short-sleeved blue shirt. She looks at another shirt. It's striped. Then Bita sees a solid green shirt. She likes it the best! She buys a medium.

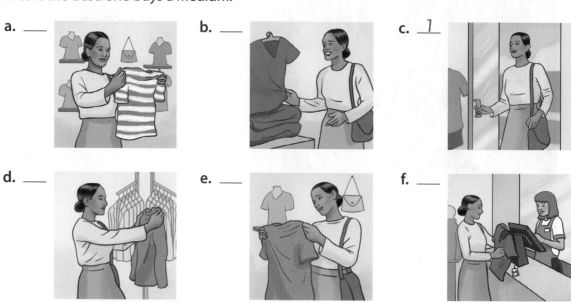

a. ____   b. ____   c. _1_

d. ____   e. ____   f. ____

4. Check (✓) the words you know. Look in your dictionary. Find the words you don't know.

Word List: Describing Clothes		
☐ heavy	☐ loose	☐ too small
☐ light	☐ narrow	☐ too big
☐ tight	☐ wide	☐ too expensive

5. Match the opposites.

a. heavy ___3___   **1.** too big

b. tight ___   **2.** narrow

c. wide ___   **3.** ~~light~~

d. too small ___   **4.** loose

6. Look at the pictures. Complete the sentences. Use the words in the box.

wide	expensive	~~light~~	small	heavy	big

a. His jacket is ___*light*___.   **b.** The shirt is too _____.   **c.** Her sweater is _____.

d. The dress is too _____.   **e.** His tie is _____.   **f.** His pants are too _____.

Making Clothes

1. **Check (✓) the words you know. Look in your dictionary. Find the words you don't know.**

Word List: Making Clothes		
☐ cotton	☐ sew	☐ pattern
☐ wool	☐ sewing machine	☐ thread
☐ leather	☐ sewing machine operator	☐ button
☐ denim	☐ needle	☐ zipper
		☐ snap

2. **Label the pictures. Use the words in the box.**

~~cotton~~	wool	leather	denim

a. ___cotton___   b. _____   c. _____   d. _____

3. **Look at the picture. Write _T_ (true) or _F_ (false).**

a. The man is using a pattern. ___T___

b. The women are sewing machine operators. ____

c. They can sew. ____

d. The man is working with leather. ____

e. The women are not sewing right now. ____

CHALLENGE Look at Exercise 2. Name two types of material you like to wear.

4. Label the picture. Write the numbers.

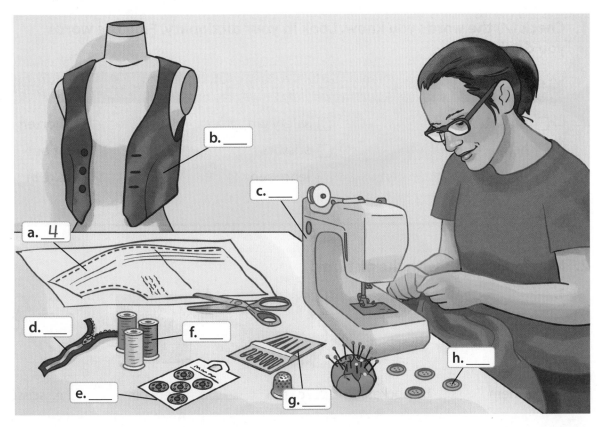

b. ____
c. ____
a. 4
d. ____
f. ____
e. ____
g. ____
h. ____

1. button   3. needle   5. sewing machine   7. thread

2. leather   4. ~~pattern~~   6. snap   8. zipper

5. Read the sentences. Check (✓) the things the people need.

a. Beatriz wants to make a dress for summer. What does she need?

    ✓ cotton material   ☐ wool

    ✓ a pattern   ✓ a sewing machine

b. Sam wants to sew a button on his shirt. What does he need?

    ☐ a pattern   ☐ a button

    ☐ thread   ☐ a needle

c. Amy needs a new zipper in her dress. What does she need?

    ☐ a sewing machine   ☐ thread

    ☐ a zipper   ☐ snaps

d. Lia wants to make jeans. What does she need?

    ☐ denim   ☐ a zipper

    ☐ a pattern   ☐ a button

Making Alterations

1. **Check (✓) the words you know. Look in your dictionary. Find the words you don't know.**

Word List: Making Alterations		
☐ pocket	☐ safety pin	☐ **shorten**
☐ hem	☐ scissors	☐ **let out**
☐ pin	☐ **lengthen**	☐ **take in**

2. **Match the words with the pictures.**

1.   2.   3.   4.   5.

__4__ **a.** hem   ____ **b.** pocket   ____ **c.** pin   ____ **d.** safety pin   ____ **e.** scissors

3. **Look at the pictures. Complete the sentences. Use the words in the box.**

lengthen	take in	let out	pocket	shorten	~~scissors~~

a. She needs a pair of
___*scissors*___.

b. She needs to
_____ the dress.

c. He needs to sew the
_____.

d. She needs to
_____ the pants.

e. He needs to
_____ the pants.

f. She needs to
_____ the dress.

1. Check (✓) the things you use and the things you do. Look in your dictionary for help.

> ### Word List: Doing the Laundry
>
> ☐ laundry   ☐ hanger   ☐ **Fold** the laundry.
>
> ☐ washer   ☐ iron   ☐ **Iron** the clothes.
>
> ☐ dryer   ☐ ironing board ☐ **Hang up** the clothes.

2. Complete the sentences. Use the words in the box.

> laundry   ~~washer~~   dryer   ironing board   hangers   fold

a. It's time to wash the clothes. Put the laundry in the ___*washer*___.

b. I need to iron my shirt. Where is the _____?

c. David and Parvin do the _____ every Saturday.

d. We need to dry the clothes. Please put the clothes in the _____.

e. Sam needs some _____. He wants to hang up his shirts.

f. The clothes in the dryer are dry. It's time to _____ the laundry.

3. Look at the story. Put the sentences in order (1-6).

____ He puts the clothes in the washer.   ____ He hangs up the shirts.

_1_ Ali needs to do the laundry.   ____ He puts the clothes in the dryer.

____ He folds some of the clothes.   ____ He irons the shirts.

A Garage Sale

1. **Check (✓) the words you know. Look in your dictionary. Find the words you don't know.**

Word List: A Garage Sale		
☐ flyer	☐ folding chair	☐ **bargain**
☐ used clothing	☐ clock radio	☐ **browse**
☐ sticker	☐ VCR	
☐ folding card table	☐ CD / cassette player	

2. **Match the words with the pictures.**

___6___ **a.** flyer

1.

_____ **b.** folding chair

2.

_____ **c.** stickers

3.

_____ **d.** VCR

4.

_____ **e.** clock radio

5.

_____ **f.** bargain

6.

_____ **g.** CD / cassette player

7.

3. **Look at the pictures. Circle the correct words.**

a. The Sanchez family has a
   clock radio /(garage sale) every year.

b. They make a flyer / sticker together.

c. They put price sales / stickers on all
   their old things.

d. They put a card table / flyer
   and two folding chairs / VCRs
   in the yard.

e. This year they have a lot of
   used clothing / stickers for sale.

f. Mr. Sanchez wants to sell an old
   VCR / clock radio.

g. Many people come to
   browse / help.

h. The customers like to
   browse / bargain with
   Mrs. Sanchez.

4. **What about you? Answer the questions. Write *Yes, I do* or *No, I don't*.**

a. Do you like to go to garage sales? _____

b. Do you like to have garage sales? _____

c. Do you like to bargain when you shop? _____

1. **Check (✓) the parts of the body that are below the neck. Look in your dictionary for help.**

Word List: The Body			
☐ head	☐ back	☐ leg	☐ shoulder
☐ hair	☐ nose	☐ toe	☐ arm
☐ neck	☐ mouth	☐ eye	☐ hand
☐ chest	☐ foot	☐ ear	☐ finger

2. **Cross out the word that doesn't belong.**

   a. eye   nose   ~~foot~~   mouth

   b. leg   neck   toe   foot

   c. back   arm   hand   finger

   d. chest   back   eye   shoulder

   e. head   hair   ear   leg

3. **Label the picture. Write the numbers.**

   1. arm
   2. back
   3. chest
   4. head
   5. eye
   6. leg
   7. ear
   8. hand
   9. ~~hair~~
   10. mouth

a. _9_   b. ___   c. ___   d. ___   e. ___   f. ___   g. ___   h. ___   i. ___   j. ___

4. Look at the picture. Read the sentences. Write the numbers.

1. Jack has a problem with his foot.
2. ~~Mary has a problem with her eye.~~
3. Rosa has a problem with her knee.

4. Sun has a problem with her back.
5. Jin has a problem with his shoulder.
6. Tej has a problem with his hand.

5. Study the graph. Answer the questions.

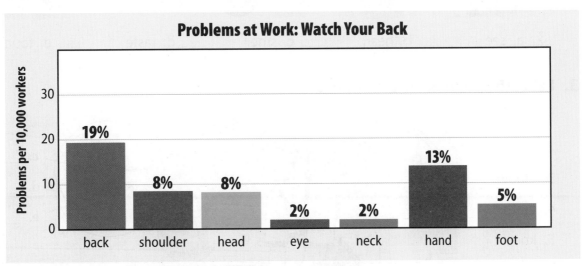

Based on information from: U.S. Bureau of Labor Statistics, 2015.

a. Nineteen percent of the problems at work are ____*back*____ problems.

b. Five percent of the problems are with the _____.

c. _____ percent of the problems are eye problems.

d. _____ percent of problems are with the shoulder and the neck.

e. Eighteen percent of problems are _____ and _____ problems.

105

Inside and Outside the Body

1. **Check (✓) the words you know. Look in your dictionary. Find the words you don't know.**

Word List: Inside and Outside the Body

The Face	The Arm	The Senses
☐ chin	☐ elbow	☐ see
☐ forehead	☐ wrist	☐ hear
The Mouth	**The Leg**	☐ smell
☐ lip	☐ knee	☐ taste
☐ teeth	☐ ankle	☐ touch
☐ tongue		

2. **Match the words with the pictures.**

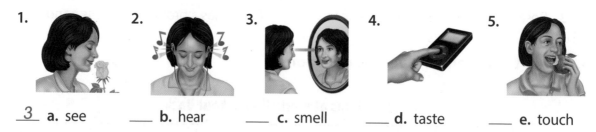

_3_ **a.** see   ___ **b.** hear   ___ **c.** smell   ___ **d.** taste   ___ **e.** touch

3. **Label the picture. Write the numbers.**

1. ankle
2. ~~chin~~
3. elbow
4. teeth
5. knee
6. lip
7. wrist
8. tongue
9. forehead

a. _2_

b. ___
c. ___
d. ___
e. ___
f. ___
g. ___
h. ___
i. ___

CHALLENGE Which senses help you learn English?

4. Check (✓) the things that are inside the chest. Look in your dictionary for help.

Word List: Inside and Outside the Body		
☐ muscle	☐ heart	☐ stomach
☐ bone	☐ lung	☐ kidney
☐ brain	☐ liver	

5. Complete the words. Write the letters.

a. h _e_ a r _t_

b. b r ___ ___ n

c. k i ___ ___ e y

d. l ___ n ___

e. l ___ ___ ___ r

f. m ___ s ___ ___ e

g. s t o ___ ___ c ___

h. b ___ ___ e

6. Look at the picture. Write T (true) or F (false).

a. The liver is above the lungs. _F_

b. The heart is between the lungs. ___

c. The lungs are in the stomach. ___

d. The brain is in the head. ___

e. There are six bones in the brain. ___

f. The liver is near the stomach. ___

g. There are two kidneys in the picture. ___

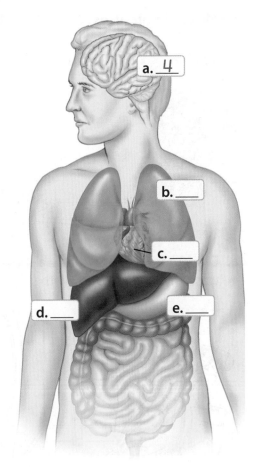

a. 4
b. ___
c. ___
d. ___
e. ___

7. Label the picture. Write the numbers.

1. heart

2. liver

3. stomach

4. ~~brain~~

5. lung

CHALLENGE   Which body part do you use to think? Which body parts do you use to breathe?

Personal Hygiene

1. **Check (✓) the things you do and the things you use every day. Look in your dictionary for help.**

Word List: Personal Hygiene		
☐ **take** a shower	☐ **put on** sunscreen	☐ **brush** hair
☐ **take** a bath	☐ **wash** hair	☐ soap
☐ **use** deodorant	☐ **dry** hair	☐ shampoo

2. **Cross out the word that doesn't belong.**

   a. wash hair   dry hair   ~~soap~~   **d.** dry   bath   shower

   b. soap   sunscreen   shampoo   **e.** wash   take   dry

   c. sunscreen   brush   deodorant   **f.** deodorant   shampoo   soap

3. **Look at the pictures. Complete the sentences. Use the words in the box.**

shampoo	soap	~~take~~	use	dry	wash

   a. Every morning I __*take*__ a shower. I wash my face and body with _____.

   b. I _____ my hair. I use my favorite _____.

   c. I _____ my hair.

   d. I _____ deodorant. Then I get dressed.

4. Check (✓) the things you do and the things you use every day. Look in your dictionary for help.

Word List: Personal Hygiene		
☐ **brush** teeth	☐ **cut** nails	☐ dental floss
☐ **floss** teeth	☐ toothbrush	☐ razor
☐ **shave**	☐ toothpaste	☐ shaving cream

5. Match the words with the pictures.

1.   2.    3.    4.    5.

_2_ **a.** toothbrush   ___ **c.** dental floss   ___ **e.** shaving cream

___ **b.** toothpaste   ___ **d.** razor

6. Complete the puzzle.

ACROSS

1. ___ your nails.

5. Use a ___ with shaving cream.

6. Use ___ with a toothbrush.

DOWN

1. Use shaving ___.

2. ___ your teeth.

3. Use dental ___.

4. Use a razor to ___.

109

Symptoms and Injuries

1. **Check (✓) the words you know. Look in your dictionary.
   Find the words you don't know.**

<table>
<tr><td colspan="3">Word List: Symptoms and Injuries</td></tr>
<tr><td>☐ headache</td><td>☐ stomachache</td><td>☐ fever</td></tr>
<tr><td>☐ toothache</td><td>☐ backache</td><td>☐ feel dizzy</td></tr>
<tr><td>☐ earache</td><td>☐ sore throat</td><td>☐ feel nauseous</td></tr>
</table>

2. **Look at the pictures. Circle the correct words.**

a. He has a (fever) /
toothache.

b. He has <u>a backache /
an earache</u>.

c. He has a <u>sore throat /
headache</u>.

d. She has a <u>sore throat /
stomachache</u>.

e. He feels <u>dizzy / nauseous</u>.

3. **Read the worker injury/illness form. Answer the questions.**

Worker Injury/Illness Form		
DATE	WORKER NAME	SYMPTOM
Feb. 11	Paul Lee	Dizzy
Feb. 24	Sue Jones	Fever / sore throat
Mar. 2	Thomas Brown	Stomachache
Mar. 5	Erica Ortiz	Headache / fever / nauseous
Mar. 30	Janet Young	Earache / sore throat
Apr. 8	Julio Ruiz	Fever / nauseous / headache
Apr. 11	Tim Emami	Backache

a. How many workers have
stomachaches? ____*one*____

b. How many workers feel
nauseous? _____

c. How many workers have
stomachaches or
headaches? _____

d. What symptom is the
same for three workers?

_____

1. Check (✓) the words you know. Look in your dictionary. Find the words you don't know.

> ### Word List: Medical Care
>
> ☐ appointment   ☐ doctor   ☐ **check** (your) blood pressure
>
> ☐ health insurance card ☐ patient   ☐ **take** (your) temperature
>
> ☐ health history form   ☐ nurse   ☐ **draw** (your) blood

2. Complete the pictures. Use all the words in the Word List.

Procedures	People	Things
a. *check your blood pressure*	d.	g.
b.	e.	h.
c.	f.	i.

3. Look at the pictures. Put the sentences in order (1–6).

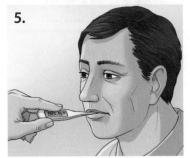

____ The nurse checks his blood pressure.   _1_ He makes an appointment to see the doctor.

____ He completes a health history form.   ____ The nurse takes his temperature.

____ He talks to the doctor.   ____ He shows his health insurance card.

Illnesses and Medical Conditions

1. **Check (✓) the illnesses and conditions that are common in your family.**

Word List: Illnesses and Medical Conditions			
☐ cold	☐ chicken pox	☐ cancer	☐ high blood pressure
☐ flu	☐ pneumonia	☐ asthma	☐ diabetes
☐ ear infection	☐ allergies	☐ arthritis	☐ heart disease
☐ measles			

2. **Cross out the word that doesn't belong.**

   a. cold ~~diabetes~~ flu

   b. high blood pressure heart disease allergies

   c. asthma ear infection diabetes

   d. heart disease chicken pox measles

   e. flu arthritis pneumonia

3. **Look at the pictures. Complete the sentences. Use the words in the box.**

arthritis ear infection	~~chicken pox~~ high blood pressure	cold pneumonia

  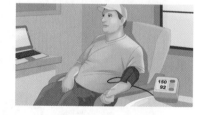

a. He has the _chicken pox_.

b. She has an _____.

c. He has _____.

d. She has _____.

e. He has a _____.

f. The patient has _____.

4. Read the medical form. Write *T* (true) or *F* (false).

MEDICAL FORM

Name: *Tom Brown*

Reason for Visit Today: *headache, sore throat, fever*

Allergies: *cats*

Vaccinations dates:

flu	*10/25/17*
chicken pox	*1991*
measles	*1991*
pneumonia	*none*

Medical History:

	Patient		Family History
	Yes	**No**	
cancer	❑	✓	*aunt, grandmother*
heart disease	❑	✓	*father*
high blood pressure	❑	✓	*father*
arthritis	❑	✓	
diabetes	❑	✓	
asthma	❑	✓	

a. Tom has asthma. <u>F</u>

b. Tom has a sore throat today. ____

c. Tom has an ear infection today. ____

d. Tom has an allergy. ____

e. Tom's father had cancer. ____

f. Tom had a measles vaccination. ____

g. Tom had a pneumonia vaccination. ____

CHALLENGE Look at Tom's symptoms. What illness do you think he has?

A Pharmacy

1. Check (✓) the medication you buy sometimes. Look in your dictionary for help.

Word List: A Pharmacy

- ☐ pharmacist
- ☐ prescription
- ☐ prescription label
- ☐ prescription number
- ☐ over-the-counter medication
- ☐ pill
- ☐ tablet
- ☐ capsule
- ☐ cream
- ☐ pain reliever
- ☐ antacid
- ☐ cough syrup
- ☐ eye drops
- ☐ nasal spray
- ☐ inhaler

2. Match the words with the definitions.

_4_ **a.** pharmacist

___ **b.** cream

___ **c.** eye drops

___ **d.** prescription

___ **e.** nasal spray

1. medication for the skin

2. medication for the eye

3. medication you get from a pharmacist

4. ~~a person who works in the pharmacy~~

5. medication for the nose

3. Look at the pictures. Circle the correct words.

a. He needs some cream / (cough syrup).

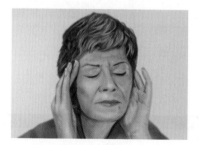

b. She needs a pain reliever / nasal spray.

c. He needs some eye drops / antacid.

d. She's using nasal spray / tablets.

e. She needs some pills / eye drops.

f. She's using an antacid / inhaler.

4. Unscramble the words.

a. pslauesc

capsules

b. emarc

_____

c. tbleats

_____

d. gucoh psury

_____

e. learhin

_____

f. phaarcistm

_____

5. Read the prescription label. Answer the questions.

a. Is this over-the-counter medication?
No, it isn't.

b. Is the prescription for pills?
_____

c. What is the prescription number?
_____

d. How many capsules does Maria take in one day?
_____

e. How many capsules does she take in one week?
_____

CDS PHARMACY Rx
225 Lind St.
Chicago, IL 60603
217-555-8578

PRESCRIPTION # 16220197
DATE: 07/17/08

TAKE TWO CAPSULES WITH
FOOD 3 TIMES A DAY
FOR STOMACH PAIN.

REFILLS: 3
PATIENT NAME: MARIA JONES

1. Check (✓) the things you do when you're sick. Look in your dictionary for help.

Word List: Taking Care of Your Health

☐ **Get** bed rest. ☐ **Stay** fit. ☐ **Have** regular checkups.

☐ **Drink** fluids. ☐ **Eat** a healthy diet. ☐ **Get** immunized.

☐ **Take** medicine. ☐ **Don't** smoke.

2. Match the words with the sentences.

_3_ **a.** Get   **1.** regular checkups.

___ **b.** Take   **2.** a healthy diet.

___ **c.** Eat   **3.** ~~immunized.~~

___ **d.** Have   **4.** rest.

___ **e.** Get bed   **5.** fluids.

___ **f.** Drink   **6.** medicine.

3. Study the graph. Answer the questions.

a. What percent of people stay fit?

_22%_

b. What percent of people eat a healthy diet?

_____

c. What percent of people don't smoke?

_____

d. What percent of people don't stay fit?

_____

e. What percent of people stay fit, eat a healthy diet, and don't smoke?

_____

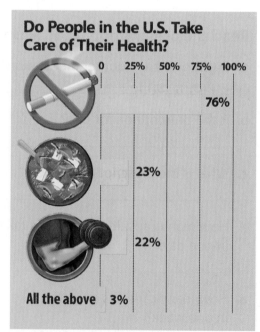

Do People in the U.S. Take Care of Their Health?

76%

23%

22%

All the above 3%

Based on information from:
US News and World Report

CHALLENGE   Name one way you take care of your health every day.

4. Check (✓) the words you know. Look in your dictionary. Find the words you don't know.

Word List: Taking Care of Your Health		
☐ vision problems	☐ stress	☐ glasses
☐ hearing loss	☐ depression	☐ hearing aid
☐ pain	☐ optometrist	☐ therapy

5. Look at the pictures. Check (✓) the correct sentences.

 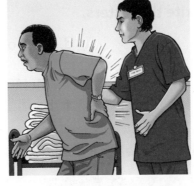 

a. ☑ She has hearing loss. **b.** ☐ He has vision problems. **c.** ☐ She's an optometrist.
   ☐ She needs glasses.   ☐ He has back pain.   ☐ He's getting a hearing aid.

6. Read the doctor's advice. Circle the correct words.

a. The problem is depression / ⟨stress⟩ at work.

b. It's important to take care of your health / therapy.

c. The doctor gives three / four ideas for help.

d. One of the doctor's ideas is pain / therapy.

e. People with a lot of stress sometimes have depression / work.

Health Advice by Dr. Bob

Dear Dr. Bob,
I have too much stress at work. I can't sleep and I feel sad all the time. What can I do to feel better?
                Stressed Out in San Diego

Dear Stressed,
Doctors know that stress can cause depression. You need to take care of your health now. Therapy, exercise, and a healthy diet can help.

CHALLENGE Name another way to take care of stress and depression.

Medical Emergencies

1. Check (✓) the words you know. Look in your dictionary. Find the words you don't know.

Word List: Medical Emergencies		
☐ ambulance	☐ **have** a heart attack	☐ **choke**
☐ paramedic	☐ **burn** (your)self	☐ **bleed**
☐ **be** hurt	☐ **drown**	☐ **break** a bone

2. Complete the words. Write the letters.

a. p _a_ ra _m_ e _d_ ic

b. be h __ __ t

c. b __ __ n y __ __ rs __ __ f

d. c __ o __ __

e. __ __ b __ l a n __ e

f. b __ __ a __ a __ o n __

3. Look at the picture. Write *T* (true) or *F* (false).

a. The girl is bleeding.   _T_

b. Two people are hurt.   __

c. The paramedics are in the ambulance.   __

d. One paramedic is having a heart attack.   __

e. The girl is choking.   __

f. One paramedic is drowning.   __

1. Check (✓) the things you have at home. Look in your dictionary for help.

Word List: First Aid

☐ first aid kit ☐ adhesive bandage ☐ gauze ☐ stitches

☐ first aid manual ☐ sterile tape ☐ ice pack ☐ CPR

☐ tweezers

2. Look at the pictures. Unscramble the sentences.

a. *She has a first aid kit.*

first aid   kit.   a   has   She

b. _____

has   He   stitches.   three

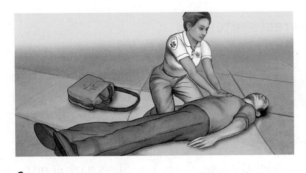

c. _____

woman   giving   The   CPR.   is

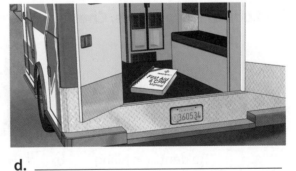

d. _____

ambulance.   in   first   aid   The   is
manual   the

3. Label the picture. Write the numbers.

1. first aid manual

2. tweezers

3. adhesive bandages

4. ice pack

5. ~~gauze~~

6. sterile tape

a. *5*

b. ____

c. ____

d. ____

e. ____

f. ____

Dental Care

1. Check (✓) the words you know. Look in your dictionary. Find the words you don't know.

Word List: Dental Care		
☐ dentist	☐ filling	☐ **clean** the teeth
☐ dental hygienist	☐ crown	☐ **take** X-rays
☐ cavity	☐ gum disease	☐ **fill** a cavity

2. Cross out the word that doesn't belong.

a. take X-rays   clean the teeth   ~~gum disease~~

b. crown   dentist   dental hygienist

c. cavity   dentist   gum disease

d. crown   filling   clean the teeth

e. fill a cavity   dental hygienist   clean the teeth

3. Look at the pictures. Check (✓) the correct sentences.

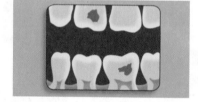

a. ☐ The dentist is filling a cavity.

☑ The patient is getting a new crown.

b. ☐ This is gum disease.

☐ There are two cavities.

c. ☐ She's a hygienist.

☐ It's a new crown.

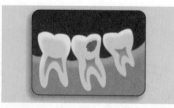

d. ☐ The patient needs a filling.

☐ The patient needs an X-ray.

e. ☐ He's a dentist.

☐ He's taking X-rays.

f. ☐ She has gum disease.

☐ She has good dental care.

1. **Check (✓) the words you know. Look in your dictionary. Find the words you don't know.**

> ### Word List: Health Insurance
>
> ☐ carrier ☐ insurance policy ☐ premium
>
> ☐ insurance plans ☐ insured ☐ co-pay
>
> ☐ benefits ☐ dependents ☐ **compare** plans

2. **Match the words with the pictures.**

1.

2.

3.

4.

_3_ **a.** insured

____ **c.** insurance policy

____ **b.** carrier

____ **d.** dependents

3. **Study the chart. Compare the plans and complete the sentences. Use the words in the box.**

> insurance plans benefits premium co-pay ~~carrier~~

a. LiveWell is an insurance ___*carrier*___.

b. LiveWell has three _____.

c. The Bronze Plan has a low _____.

d. The _____ for the Silver Plan is $25.

e. The Gold Plan has good _____, but it's expensive.

LiveWell Insurance Company			
	Bronze	Silver	Gold
Monthly Premium	$	$$	$$$
Co-Pay	$45	$25	none

CHALLENGE Where can you find information about health insurance? Find a website for your state.

1. Check (✓) the doctors you go to. Look in your dictionary for help.

Word List: A Hospital

☐ internist   ☐ pediatrician   ☐ nursing assistant

☐ obstetrician   ☐ psychiatrist   ☐ orderly

☐ cardiologist   ☐ nurse

2. Match the words with the definitions.

_5_ **a.** psychiatrist

____ **b.** nurse

____ **c.** internist

____ **d.** pediatrician

____ **e.** cardiologist

____ **f.** obstetrician

1. a doctor for children

2. a doctor for heart problems

3. a doctor for pregnant women

4. a doctor for general problems

5. ~~a doctor for depression and stress~~

6. a person who helps patients and doctors

3. Look at the pictures. Read the sentences. Number the people.

_2_ **a.**

____ **b.**

____ **c.**

____ **d.**

____ **e.**

____ **f.**

1. Dr. Aziz is a pediatrician.

2. ~~Tanya Orloff is a nursing assistant.~~

3. Dr. Kumar is a cardiologist.

4. Dr. Chen is an obstetrician.

5. Ms. Hart is a nurse.

6. Luis Ramos is an orderly.

4. Check (✓) the things in a hospital room. Look in your dictionary for help.

Word List: A Hospital		
☐ patient	☐ hospital bed	☐ call button
☐ hospital gown	☐ medical chart	☐ blood work
☐ medication	☐ IV	

5. Label the pictures. Use the words in the box.

call button   IV   hospital bed   ~~medical chart~~   patient   blood work

a. _medical chart_

b. _____

c. _____

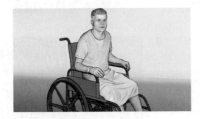

d. _____

e. _____

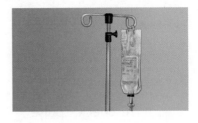

f. _____

6. Read the story. Circle the correct words.

a. Kim is in the (hospital) / patient.

b. She puts on a hospital gown / call button.

c. The nurse gives Kim some hospital / medication.

d. He reads Kim's hospital bed / medical chart.

e. Kim needs some blood work / call button.

123

A Health Fair

1. **Check (✓) the words you know. Look in your dictionary. Find the words you don't know.**

Word List: A Health Fair		
☐ low-cost exam	☐ aerobic exercise	☐ nutrition label
☐ acupuncture	☐ demonstration	☐ **check** (your) pulse
☐ booth	☐ sugar-free	☐ **give** a lecture
☐ yoga		

2. **Match the words with the pictures.**

    _8_ **a.** booth

    ___ **b.** give a lecture

    ___ **c.** low-cost exam

    ___ **d.** aerobic exercise

    ___ **e.** nutrition label

    ___ **f.** yoga

    ___ **g.** acupuncture

    ___ **h.** check...pulse

    1.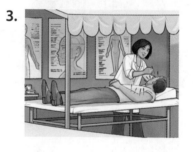

    2.

    3.

    4.

    5.

    6.

    7.

    8.

3. Look at the pictures. Circle the correct words.

a. Pam is at the (health fair) / exam.

b. There are many nutrition labels / booths to visit.

c. First, she goes to the exercise demonstration / lecture about nutrition labels.

d. Pam wants to get more sugar-free food / exercise.

e. She watches the yoga / acupuncture demonstration.

f. Pam eats a healthy lunch. Then she gets a low-cost exam / nutrition label.

g. A nurse takes Pam's blood pressure and booth / pulse.

h. Pam is having a great day at the sugar-free / health fair.

4. What about you? How often do you do these healthy things?

	Every Week	Every Year	Never
I read nutrition labels . . .			
I have a medical exam . . .			
I do aerobic exercises . . .			

1. Check (✓) the places you go every week.

Word List: Downtown

☐ parking garage ☐ police station ☐ post office

☐ office building ☐ bus station ☐ fire station

☐ hotel ☐ city hall ☐ courthouse

☐ Department of Motor Vehicles ☐ hospital ☐ restaurant

☐ bank ☐ gas station ☐ library

2. Match the words.

_2_ **a.** city   **1.** garage

___ **b.** post   **2.** ~~hall~~

___ **c.** bus   **3.** Motor Vehicles

___ **d.** parking   **4.** station

___ **e.** office   **5.** office

___ **f.** Department of   **6.** building

3. Read the sentences. Write *T* (true) or *F* (false).

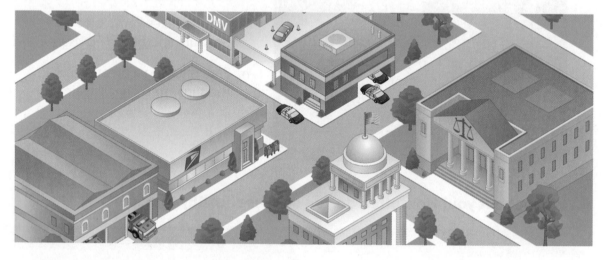

a. There are mailboxes at the post office. _T_

b. There are police cars at the fire station. ___

c. You can take a driving test at the Department of Motor Vehicles. ___

d. You can buy gas at city hall. ___

e. You can sleep at the courthouse. ___

f. There are police cars at the police station. ___

4. Complete the sentences. Use the words in the box.

hospital	library	restaurant	~~parking garage~~
gas station	hotel	post office	office building

a. Roberto wants to park his car.
   He's looking for a _parking garage_ .

b. Mrs. Smith is going to have a baby.
   They're going to the _____.

c. Mr. Tran is visiting New York.
   He's going to a _____.

d. Fran needs stamps.
   She's at the _____.

e. Rosa has a business meeting. She's
   going to an _____.

f. Bill needs gas for his car.
   He's at the _____.

g. Elda is hungry.
   She's at a _____.

h. Mr. Patel wants some books.
   He's going to the _____.

5. Think about where you live. Answer the questions.

a. Is there a bank downtown?   _____

b. Is there a library downtown?   _____

c. Do you like to go downtown?   _____

1. Check (✓) the places you like. Look in your dictionary for help.

> **Word List: City Streets**
>
> ☐ stadium   ☐ school   ☐ synagogue
> ☐ factory   ☐ gym   ☐ community college
> ☐ mosque   ☐ coffee shop   ☐ supermarket
> ☐ movie theater ☐ motel   ☐ bakery
> ☐ shopping mall ☐ church

2. Cross out the word that doesn't belong.

a. ~~motel~~   coffee shop   bakery

b. school   shopping mall   community college

c. movie theater   stadium   factory

d. supermarket   motel   bakery

e. gym   church   synagogue

3. Label the picture. Use the words in the box.

> gym   motel   coffee shop   community college   school   ~~supermarket~~

a. _supermarket_

b. _____

c. _____

d. _____

e. _____

f. _____

4. Look at the pictures. Check (✓) the correct sentences.

a. ✓ They're at the movie theater.

☐ They're at the stadium.

b. ☐ He's at school.

☐ He's at the gym.

c. ☐ They're at the coffee shop.

☐ They're at the shopping mall.

d. ☐ The mosque is white.

☐ The church is brown.

e. ☐ She works at the motel.

☐ She works at the supermarket.

f. ☐ He's at the factory.

☐ He's at the bakery.

5. Study the bus schedule. Answer the questions. Write *yes* or *no*.

a. Tim is at the mall. He's going to the stadium.
Can he take this bus? _____ yes _____

b. Sharon lives on Main Street. She has a class
at 12:15. Can she take this bus? _____

c. It's 12:00. Mary is at the community college.
She wants to see a movie at 12:30.
Can she take this bus? _____

🚌 CITY CENTER	BUS SCHEDULE
STOPS	**TIMES**
Main Street	11:45 a.m.
City Community College	12:05 p.m.
3rd Street Mall	12:15 p.m.
Baker Street	12:30 p.m.
Center Movie Theater	12:40 p.m.
Front Street Stadium	1:00 p.m.

An Intersection

1. Check (✓) the places and things you see every day. Look in your dictionary for help.

Word List: An Intersection		
☐ laundromat	☐ corner	☐ crosswalk
☐ dry cleaners	☐ traffic light	☐ bus stop
☐ convenience store	☐ bus	☐ bike
☐ pharmacy	☐ mailbox	☐ sidewalk
☐ parking space	☐ pedestrian	☐ parking meter

2. Write the words in the chart. Use the words in the box.

sidewalk	dry cleaners	~~convenience store~~
crosswalk	pharmacy	

	Places to Go		Places for Pedestrians
a.	convenience store	d.	
b.		e.	
c.			

3. What's wrong with the picture? Circle the correct words.

a. The (traffic lights)/ mailboxes are different colors.

b. A bus / traffic light is blue.

c. A pedestrian / car is in the crosswalk.

d. The pedestrians are in the mailbox / intersection.

e. The car is in two parking meters / parking spaces.

f. The bus is on the sidewalk / in the intersection.

4. Look at the picture. Read the sentences. Write the numbers.

1. Irma is in the crosswalk.

2. Hari is on the sidewalk.

3. Joe is on the corner of Main and Green Street.

4. ~~Fred is in front of the laundromat.~~

5. Mary is at the parking meter.

6. Bella is at the bus stop.

5. Look at the chart. Answer the questions.

a. How many people drive a car?   <u>45</u> %

b. How many people ride the bus?   _____%

c. How many people are pedestrians?   _____%

d. How many people ride bikes?   _____%

e. How many people aren't pedestrians? _____%

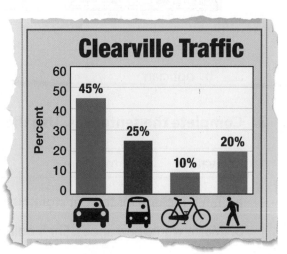

CHALLENGE   Do you think it's easy or difficult to find a parking space in Clearville?

A Mall

1. Check (✓) the places you like to shop. Look in your dictionary for help.

Word List: A Mall		
☐ music store	☐ pet store	☐ food court
☐ jewelry store	☐ card store	☐ hair salon
☐ nail salon	☐ optician	☐ elevator
☐ bookstore	☐ shoe store	☐ escalator
☐ toy store	☐ department store	☐ directory

2. Match the words with the pictures.

1.
2.
3.

4.
5.
6.

_4_ **a.** bookstore   ___ **c.** music store   ___ **e.** department store

___ **b.** optician   ___ **d.** hair salon   ___ **f.** jewelry store

3. Complete the sentences. Use the words in the box.

elevator	toy store	~~directory~~	shoe store	card store

a. Tan is looking for the pet store. He needs a _____ _directory_ _____.

b. Marta wants new shoes. She's going to the _____.

c. Frank wants to go to the second floor. He needs an _____.

d. Billy wants a new ball. He's looking for the _____.

e. Diana is buying a birthday card for her friend. She's at the _____.

4. Study the map and the directory. Write *T* (true) or *F* (false).

a. There's a department store in the mall.　　_T_

b. There's an optician in the mall.　　___

c. The directory shows six stores.　　___

d. The food court is next to the nail salon.　　___

e. There's an escalator near the food court.　　___

f. Hair Today is a toy store.　　___

g. Tammi's is a pet store.　　___

h. The music store is next to the bookstore.　　___

5. What about you? Answer the questions.

a. Do you like to shop at the mall?　　_____

b. Is there a mall near your home?　　_____

c. Name three kinds of stores you like.　　_____

The Bank

1. Check (✓) the words you know. Look in your dictionary. Find the words you don't know.

> ### Word List: The Bank
>
> ☐ teller   ☐ ATM card   ☐ balance
>
> ☐ customer   ☐ checking account number   ☐ **Cash** a check.
>
> ☐ checkbook   ☐ bank statement   ☐ **Make** a deposit.

2. Look at the pictures. Write _T_ (true) or _F_ (false).

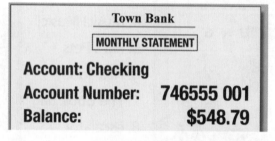

a. It's a bank statement. <u>T</u>

b. The checking account number is 746555 001. ____

c. The balance is $465.55. ____

d. The customer is cashing a check. ____

e. The customer has an ATM card. ____

f. The customer is making a deposit. ____

g. They're new customers. ____

h. They're getting a check book. ____

i. The bank manager is talking to tellers. ____

3. Complete the story. Use the words in the box.

> ~~customer~~   teller   deposit   ATM card   balance

Ingrid is a <u>customer</u> at State Bank. She makes a _____ every Friday.
                a.   **b.**

She talks to a _____ or she uses her _____. Her _____ is $1,200.00.
             c.   **d.**   **e.**

1. **Check (✓) the words you know. Look in your dictionary. Find the words you don't know.**

Word List: The Library

☐ **get** a library card   ☐ **pay** a late fine   ☐ title

☐ **look for** a book   ☐ library clerk   ☐ author

☐ **check out** a book   ☐ picture book   ☐ e-book

☐ **return** a book

2. **Look at the pictures. Read the sentences. Write the numbers.**

_6_ **a.**    ___ **b.**    ___ **c.**

___ **d.**    ___ **e.**    ___ **f.**

1. Talk to a library clerk.   **3.** Get a library card.   **5.** Look for a book.

2. Return a book.   **4.** Pay a late fine.   **6.** ~~Check out a book~~.

3. **Look at the book. Circle the correct words.**

a. The <u>author / title</u> is _The Big Red Truck_.

b. Emma Aims is the <u>author / title</u>.

c. It is <u>an e-book / a picture book</u>.

135

The Post Office

1. Check (✓) the words you know. Look in your dictionary. Find the words you don't know.

Word List: The Post Office		
☐ postal clerk	☐ package	☐ stamp
☐ letter	☐ book of stamps	☐ **Address** the envelope.
☐ envelope	☐ letter carrier	☐ **Put on** a stamp.
☐ greeting card	☐ return address	☐ **Mail** the card.
☐ post card	☐ mailing address	

2. Cross out the word that doesn't belong.

a. letter carrier ~~stamp~~ postal clerk

b. return address mailing address book of stamps

c. post office package letter

d. greeting card post card postal clerk

e. Address the envelope. greeting card Put on a stamp.

3. Complete the story. Use the words in the box.

address	~~greeting~~	envelope	stamp
post office	return	mails	book

a. Mira buys a _greeting_ card at the card shop.

b. She puts the card in an _____.

c. She writes the mailing _____ and the _____ address on the envelope.

d. Then she buys a _____ of stamps at the _____.

e. She puts a _____ on the envelope.

f. She _____ the card.

4. Look at the picture. Write _T_ (true) or _F_ (false).

a. Luz is a postal clerk. _T_

b. The customer is mailing an envelope. ____

c. Larry is a postal clerk. ____

d. Larry carries cards, letters, post cards, and packages. ____

e. You can buy stamps for post cards at the post office. ____

f. You can buy stamps for letters at the post office. ____

5. Read the information. Complete the envelope.

Anna Rojas is mailing the letter. Her address is 22 Main Street, Los Angeles, CA 90020

The letter is going to Frank Rojas. His address is 919 Glad Street, Miami, FL 33136.

a. Write Anna's address on the envelope.

b. Write Frank's address on the envelope.

c. Draw a stamp on the envelope.

Department of Motor Vehicles (DMV)

1. Check (✓) the things you get at the DMV. Look in your dictionary for help.

Word List: Department of Motor Vehicles (DMV)

☐ DMV clerk ☐ window ☐ driver's license number

☐ photo ☐ proof of insurance ☐ license plate

☐ fingerprint ☐ driver's license ☐ registration sticker

☐ vision exam

2. Label the pictures. Write the numbers.

_3_ a.  ___ b.  ___ c.

___ d.  ___ e.  ___ f.

1. registration sticker   3. ~~license plate~~   5. driver's license

2. driver's license number   4. photo   6. fingerprint

3. Look at the picture. Circle the correct words.

a. Mario is at the photo / (DMV).

b. He needs a new driver's license / window.

c. He goes to the window / stickers.

d. He talks to a registration / clerk.

e. He gets a proof of insurance / vision exam.

f. The clerk takes his license number / fingerprints and his photo / license plate.

4. Put the steps in order (1-5). Look in your dictionary for help.

Word List: Department of Motor Vehicles (DMV)
___ **Get** your license.   ___ **Pay** the application fee.   ___ **Take** a written test.
___ **Pass** a driving test.   _1_ **Take** a driver education course.

5. Look at the pictures. Complete the story. Use the words in the box.

~~driver's license~~	written test	proof of insurance
driving test	driver education course	application fee

a. Elena is getting her _driver's license_ .

b. She takes a _____ .

c. She pays the _____ .

d. She takes a _____ .

e. She shows _____ .

f. She passes the _____ .

Government and Military Service

1. **Check (✓) the words you know. Look in your dictionary. Find the words you don't know.**

> ## Word List: Government and Military Service
>
> ### National Government
>
> **Legislative Branch**
> - ☐ U.S. Capitol
> - ☐ Congress
>
> **Executive Branch**
> - ☐ White House
> - ☐ president
>
> **Judicial Branch**
> - ☐ Supreme Court
> - ☐ chief justice
>
> ### State Government
> - ☐ governor
> - ☐ state capital
> - ☐ Legislature
>
> ### City Government
> - ☐ mayor
> - ☐ city council
> - ☐ council person

2. **Circle the correct words.**

   a. The ⟨chief justice⟩/ mayor is part of the judicial branch of government.

   b. Congress works in the <u>U.S. Capitol / White House</u>.

   c. The president lives in the <u>state capitol / White House</u>.

   d. The national government and the state governments have a <u>president / legislature</u>.

3. **Complete the sentences. Use the words in the box.**

> | city | city council | state capital | governor | councilperson | ~~government~~ |

   a. The governor is part of the state ___*government*___.

   b. The governor lives and works in the _____.

   c. The Legislature and the _____ work together.

   d. The mayor is part of _____ government.

   e. The mayor works with the _____.

   f. Every _____ on the city council is important.

4. Check (✓) the words for people. Look in your dictionary for help.

Word List: Government and Military Service			
☐ officer	☐ Army	☐ Air Force	☐ Coast Guard
☐ be on active duty	☐ soldier	☐ airman	☐ coast guardsmen
☐ be on reserve	☐ Navy	☐ Marines	
☐ be a veteran	☐ sailor	☐ marine	

5. Match the person to the branch of the military.

<u>2</u> **a.** Air Force

1. sailor

____ **b.** Army

2. ~~airman~~

____ **c.** Coast Guard

3. marine

____ **d.** Marines

4. soldier

____ **e.** Navy

5. coast guardsman

6. Look at the pictures. Complete the sentences. Use the words in the box.

active	officer	reserve	~~soldier~~	veteran

a. The ___*soldier*___ listens to the
_____.

b. She is a student, but sometimes the Army
calls her. She is on _____.

c. My grandfather is a _____.
He was in the Marines.

d. My brother is in the Air Force. He's on
_____ duty in Europe right
now.

Civic Engagement

1. Check (✓) your rights and responsibilities. Look in your dictionary for help.

Word List: Civic Engagement		
Responsibilities	**Citizenship Requirements**	**Rights**
☐ **vote**	☐ **live** in the U.S. for 5 years	☐ free speech
☐ **pay** taxes	☐ **take** a citizenship test	☐ freedom of religion
☐ **obey** the law		☐ a fair trial
☐ **serve** on a jury		

2. Match the words.

_3_ **a.** pay   **1.** a citizenship test

___ **b.** live   **2.** the law

___ **c.** take   **3.** ~~taxes~~

___ **d.** obey   **4.** on a jury

___ **e.** serve   **5.** in the U.S.

3. Look at the pictures. Check (✓) the correct sentences.

a.

☑ They have freedom of religion.
☐ They have the right to a fair trial.

b.

☐ He's going to vote.
☐ He's going to pay taxes.

c.

☐ She's taking a citizenship test.
☐ She has the right to free speech.

d.

☐ He's paying taxes.
☐ He has the right to a fair trial.

4. Check (✓) the words you know. Look in your dictionary. Find the words you don't know.

Word List: Civic Engagement		
☐ **run for** office	☐ **get elected**	☐ opponent
☐ **campaign**	☐ candidate	☐ ballot
☐ **debate**	☐ rally	☐ election results

5. Look at the pictures. Circle the correct words.

a. Loretta Perez is running for ballot / office.

b. John Thompson is also a candidate / ballot.

c. He is Loretta's opponent / rally.

d. Perez and Thompson campaign / debate for two months.

e. Perez and Thompson debate / get elected twice.

f. People come to ballots / rallies for Perez and Thompson.

g. On Election Day, the voters complete their candidate / ballots.

h. The next day, everyone sees the election offices / results.

i. Perez runs / gets elected! She's very happy.

1. Check (✓) the words you know. Look in your dictionary. Find the words you don't know.

Word List: The Legal System		
☐ police officer	☐ jury	☐ **hire** a lawyer
☐ defendant	☐ witness	☐ **go** to jail
☐ judge	☐ **arrest** a suspect	☐ **be** released

2. Label the pictures. Use the words in the box.

jury	~~judge~~	witness	lawyer	jail	police officer

a. _____judge_____

b. _____

c. _____

d. _____

e. _____

f. _____

3. Read the sentences. Write _T_ (true) or _F_ (false).

a. A police officer can arrest a suspect. _T_

b. A defendant can hire a lawyer. ___

c. A suspect can arrest a police officer. ___

d. A defendant can go to jail or be released. ___

e. A defendant can hire a judge. ___

f. A judge can talk to a lawyer. ___

**1. Check (✓) the words you know. Look in your dictionary.
Find the words you don't know.**

Word List: Crime		
☐ vandalism	☐ shoplifting	☐ mugging
☐ burglary	☐ identity theft	☐ murder
☐ drunk driving	☐ victim	☐ gun

2. Unscramble the words.

a. ugn g _u_ _n_

b. durmer m __ r __ __ r

c. tmivic __ __ c __ __ m

d. gugingm __ __ g g __ __ g

e. largybur b __ __ g __ __ __ y

f. nkrud divirng __ r __ __ k d __ __ v __ __ __ __

3. Label the pictures. Use the words in the box.

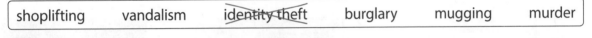

shoplifting   vandalism   ~~identity theft~~   burglary   mugging   murder

a. _identity theft_   **b.** _____   **c.** _____

d. _____   **e.** _____   **f.** _____

Public Safety

1. Check (✓) the things you do to be safe. Look in your dictionary for help.

Word List: Public Safety

☐ **Walk** with a friend.

☐ **Protect** your purse or wallet.

☐ **Lock** your doors.

☐ Don't **drink** and **drive**.

☐ **Report** crimes to the police.

☐ **Join** a Neighborhood Watch.

2. Unscramble the sentences.

a. your Lock doors.   *Lock your doors.*

b. friend. a Walk with   _____

c. your Protect purse.   _____

d. Watch. a Neighborhood Join   _____

e. crimes the Report to police.   _____

3. Look at the story. Put the sentences in order (1–6).

1.

2.

3.

4.

5.
I need to report a crime.

6.

___ This evening, they see a problem.

_1_ Lidia and Carla lock their doors.

___ They report the crime to the police.

___ They walk together in the evening.

___ They join a neighborhood watch.

___ They know it's a crime to drink and drive.

1. Check (✓) the words you know. Look in your dictionary. Find the words you don't know.

> ### Word List: Cyber Safety
>
> ☐ **Turn on** parental controls. ☐ **Create** secure passwords. ☐ cyberbullying
>
> ☐ **Monitor** children's Internet use. ☐ **Update** security software. ☐ hacking
>
> ☐ **Block** inappropriate sites. ☐ **Delete** suspicious emails.

2. Match the parts of the sentence.

_2_ **a.** Block   **1.** suspicious emails.

___ **b.** Update   **2.** ~~inappropriate sites.~~

___ **c.** Delete   **3.** parental controls.

___ **d.** Turn on   **4.** security software.

___ **e.** Monitor   **5.** secure passwords.

___ **f.** Create   **6.** children's Internet use.

3. Look at the pictures. Complete the sentences. Use the words in the box.

> block   cyberbullying   monitor   hacking   ~~create~~   turn on

a. ___*Create*___ secure passwords. Don't use your birthdate!

b. _____ is a crime. Now he is going to jail.

c. You can _____ parental controls and _____ inappropriate sites.

d. _____ is a problem for many children. _____ your children's Internet use.

Emergencies and Natural Disasters

1. **Check (✓) the emergencies and disasters. Look in your dictionary for help.**

Word List: Emergencies and Natural Disasters

☐ lost child   ☐ airplane crash   ☐ earthquake   ☐ firefighter

☐ car accident   ☐ explosion   ☐ fire   ☐ fire truck

2. **Cross out the word that doesn't belong.**

a. car accident   ~~earthquake~~   airplane crash

b. explosion   fire   lost child

c. earthquake   firefighter   fire truck

d. earthquake   natural disaster   car accident

e. lost child   firefighter   crash

3. **Look at the pictures. Complete the story. Use the words in the box.**

fire   ~~firefighters~~   fire truck   lost child   explosion

a. Police officers and ___*firefighters*___ fight a _____.

b. An _____ started the fire at 7:00 p.m.

c. The first _____ arrived at 7:06.

d. Officer Tim Juarez helps a _____ find her family.

CHALLENGE   Do the pictures show an emergency, a natural disaster, or both?

148

4. **Check (✓) the disasters that happen in your country. Look in your dictionary for help.**

Word List: Emergencies and Natural Disasters			
☐ drought	☐ blizzard	☐ tornado	☐ flood
☐ famine	☐ hurricane	☐ tsunami	

5. **Match the words with the same idea.**

___4___ **a.** hurricane   **1.** a lot of snow

_____ **b.** famine   **2.** too much water

_____ **c.** drought   **3.** no rain

_____ **d.** flood   **4.** ~~wind and rain~~

_____ **e.** blizzard   **5.** no food

6. **Study the map. Write *T* (true) or *F* (false).**

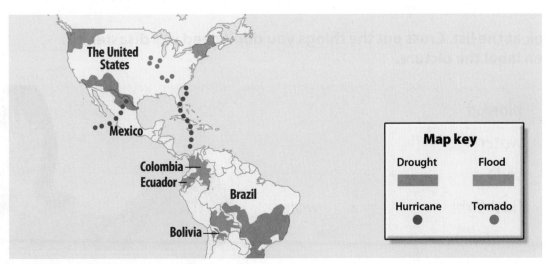

a. There are hurricanes in Brazil and Colombia.   _F_

b. There is drought in the U.S. and Mexico.   ___

c. There are floods in Bolivia.   ___

d. There are hurricanes, tornadoes, and floods in the United States.   ___

e. There are blizzards in Mexico.   ___

f. There are tsunamis in Brazil.   ___

CHALLENGE   Think about world weather. Name a natural disaster from this year.

Emergency Procedures

1. Check (✓) the things you have at home. Look in your dictionary for help.

Word List: Emergency Procedures

- ☐ **Make** a disaster kit.
- ☐ warm clothes
- ☐ blankets
- ☐ can opener
- ☐ canned food
- ☐ bottled water
- ☐ flashlight
- ☐ batteries
- ☐ first aid kit

2. What do you need in a disaster kit? Match the words.

_2_ **a.** first aid

___ **b.** canned

___ **c.** bottled

___ **d.** warm

___ **e.** can

1. clothes

2. ~~kit~~

3. opener

4. food

5. water

3. Look at the list. Cross out the things you don't need in a disaster kit. Then label the picture.

blanket

water

~~soda~~

flashlight

sandwiches

canned food

first aid kit

can opener

DVR player

new shoes

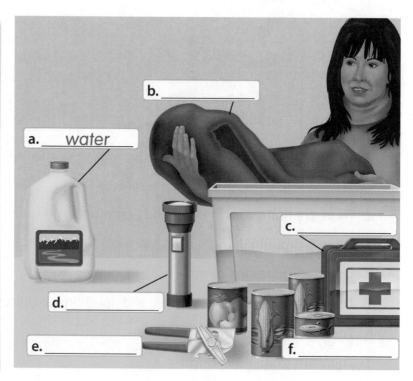

a. water

b. _____

c. _____

d. _____

e. _____

f. _____

CHALLENGE Name three other things you need in a disaster kit.

4. Check (✓) the things you know how to do. Look in your dictionary for help.

Word List: Emergency Procedures		
☐ **Watch** the weather.	☐ **Remain** calm.	☐ **Clean up** debris.
☐ **Pay attention** to warnings.	☐ **Follow** directions.	☐ **Inspect** utilities.

5. Unscramble the sentences.

a. watch the They weather.   *They watch the weather.*

b. calm. They remain   _____

c. attention to warnings. pay They   _____

d. up debris. the They clean   _____

e. the inspect They utilities.   _____

6. Look at the pictures. Circle the correct words.

Hurricane Watch

a. Sue is watching the (weather) / debris.

b. Jose is <u>inspecting / paying attention to</u> the radio.

c. The <u>warnings / utilities</u> say to leave the area.

d. The family remains <u>at home / calm</u>.

e. They follow <u>directions / attention</u>.

f. They go home later and <u>watch / clean up</u> the debris.

g. They inspect the <u>debris / utilities</u>. Everything is fine.

1. Check (✓) the words you know. Look in your dictionary. Find the words you don't know.

Word List: Community Cleanup		
☐ graffiti	☐ hardware store	☐ **give** a speech
☐ litter	☐ petition	☐ **applaud**
☐ streetlight		☐ **change**

2. Match the words with the pictures.

_5_ a.   — b.   — c.

— d.   — e.   — f.

1. litter

2. graffiti

3. petition

4. give a speech

5. ~~hardware store~~

6. applaud

3. Unscramble the sentences.

a. on There's the graffiti store. hardware   _There's graffiti on the hardware store._

b. this street. litter on There's   _____

c. streetlight The broken. is   _____

d. The petition. sign a people   _____

e. change They Center Street.   _____

4. Look at the pictures. Complete the story. Use the words in the box.

streetlight	applaud	petition	litter	community
hardware store	speech	~~graffiti~~	change	

a. There's ___graffiti___ on the hardware store and litter on the street.

b. A _____ is broken, too.

c. Sanjay owns the _____. He wants to clean up the street.

d. Many people sign a _____.

e. They plan a _____ cleanup.

f. Many people clean up the _____.

g. Everyone works together. They _____ the street together.

h. Later they have a party. Sanjay gives a _____.

i. He says, "Thank you, everyone!" All the people _____.

5. What about you? Answer the questions.

a. Does your neighborhood need a community cleanup? _____

b. What do you want to change in your neighborhood? _____

Basic Transportation

1. Check (✓) the things you use for transportation. Look in your dictionary for help.

Word List: Basic Transportation

- ☐ car
- ☐ passenger
- ☐ taxi
- ☐ motorcycle
- ☐ street

- ☐ truck
- ☐ train
- ☐ (air)plane
- ☐ helicopter
- ☐ airport

- ☐ subway station
- ☐ subway
- ☐ bus stop
- ☐ bus
- ☐ bicycle

2. Unscramble the sentences.

a. The at bus the is bus stop.   _The bus is at the bus stop._

b. subway There's station. the   _____

c. airport. is at Sam the   _____

d. driving the is Eli truck.   _____

e. is The taxi. in passenger the   _____

3. Label the pictures. Use the words in the box.

taxi   motorcycle   helicopter   ~~bicycle~~   airplane   subway

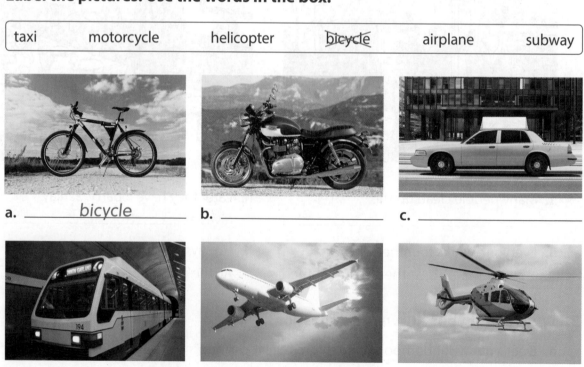

a. _____bicycle_____   b. _____   c. _____

d. _____   e. _____   f. _____

154

4. Study the chart. Answer the questions.

New York to Philadelphia		
Transportation	**Time**	**Cost**
Car	2 to 3 hours	$30.00
Bus	2 1/2 hours	$24.00
Train	2 1/2 hours	$45.50

a. Name the kinds of transportation in the chart.

  _____car_____ _____ _____

b. How much is the bus from New York to Philadelphia? _____

c. How many hours is it by train? _____

d. How many hours is it by car? _____

5. Study the graph. Complete the sentences.

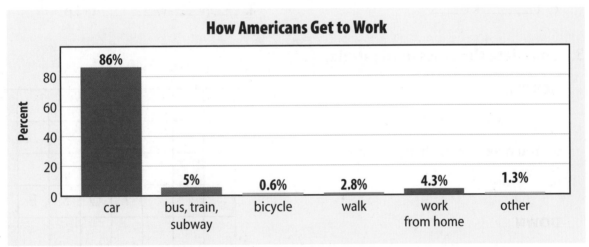

Based on information from: United States Census Bureau American Community Survey, 2008–2012.

a. Eighty-six percent of people get to work by _____car_____.

b. Five percent of people ride a train, subway, or _____.

c. Not many people ride a _____ to work.

d. A _____ is an example of other transportation.

6. What about you? Answer the questions.

a. What transportation do you use to get to work or school? _____

b. How do you travel long distances? _____

1. **Check (✓) the words you know. Look in your dictionary. Find the words you don't know.**

Word List: Public Transportation		
☐ fare	☐ token	☐ ticket
☐ schedule	☐ fare card	☐ one-way trip
☐ transfer	☐ ticket window	☐ round trip

2. **Complete the words. Write the letters.**

   a. tr _a_ n _s_ f _e_ _r_

   b. f __ __ e c __ r __

   c. t __ __ k e __

   d. t __ __ __ n

   e. s __ __ e d __ l __

   f. __ n __ -w __ __ t r i p

3. **Complete the crossword puzzle.**

   ACROSS

   2. You need this for the subway.

   5. You need this to change buses.

   6. ___ trip

   DOWN

   1. It has information about bus times and stops.

   3. bus money

   4. ticket ___

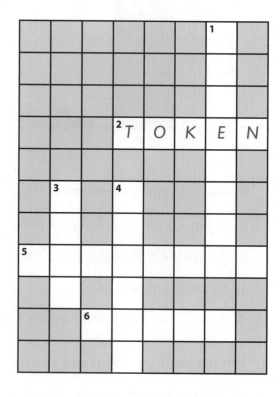

1. **Check (✓) the words you know. Look in your dictionary. Find the words you don't know.**

Word List: Prepositions of Motion		
☐ **go under** the bridge	☐ **walk down** the steps	☐ **get on** the highway
☐ **go over** the bridge	☐ **get into** the taxi	☐ **get off** the highway
☐ **walk up** the steps	☐ **get out of** the taxi	☐ **drive through** the tunnel

2. **Write the opposites. Use the words in the box.**

get out of	go over	get off	~~walk down~~	walk under

a. walk up   _walk down_   **d.** get on   _____

b. go under   _____   **e.** walk over   _____

c. get into   _____

3. **Read the sentences. Number the people.**

1. ~~Rico is walking down the steps.~~

2. Al is driving through the intersection.

3. Oscar is getting into a taxi.

4. Hansa is walking up the steps.

5. Paula is getting off the bus.

1. **Check (✓) the traffic signs you see between your home and school. Look in your dictionary for help.**

Word List: Traffic Signs		
☐ stop	☐ speed limit	☐ yield
☐ do not enter	☐ right turn only	☐ no parking
☐ one way	☐ no left turn	☐ handicapped parking

2. **Complete the signs. Use the Word List for help.**

a.
yield

b.

c.

d.

e.

f.

3. **Look at the pictures. Write _T_ (true) or _F_ (false).**

a. The car can turn right on Main Street. ___T___

b. First Street is one way. _____

c. It's OK for the purple car to turn left. _____

d. There's no parking on Main Street. _____

e. Main Street is one way. _____

[CHALLENGE] Name three traffic signs between your home and your school.

1. **Check (✓) the words you know. Look in your dictionary.
   Find the words you don't know.**

Word List: Directions and Maps			
☐ go straight	☐ turn left	☐ north	☐ south
☐ turn right	☐ stop	☐ west	☐ east

2. **Unscramble the words.**

   a. rothn __n__ __o__ __r__ th

   b. tops s __ __ __ __

   c. sewt __ e __ __

   d. eats __ __ __ t

   e. ouths s __ __ __ __ __

   f. urtn fetl __ __ __ n __ e __ __ __

3. **Label the picture with the numbers.**

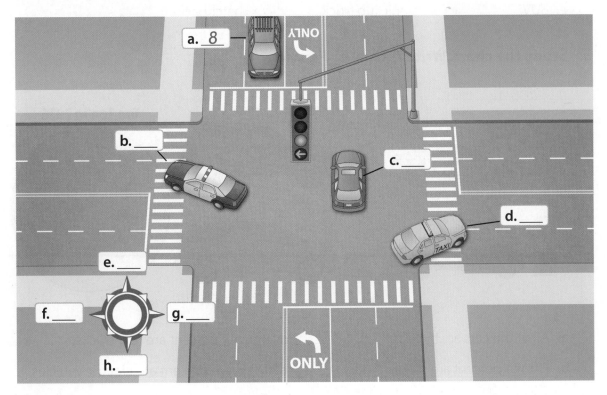

1. north
2. west
3. south
4. east
5. go straight
6. turn right
7. turn left
8. ~~stop~~

Cars and Trucks

1. **Check (✓) the cars and trucks you like. Look in your dictionary for help.**

Word List: Cars and Trucks		
☐ hybrid	☐ hatchback	☐ pickup truck
☐ electric vehicle	☐ SUV	☐ tow truck
☐ convertible	☐ minivan	☐ school bus

2. **Cross out the word that doesn't belong.**

a.	SUV	minivan	~~school bus~~
b.	electric vehicle	convertible	hybrid
c.	tow truck	convertible	hatchback
d.	pickup truck	tow truck	hybrid
e.	SUV	pickup truck	hatchback

3. **Study the chart. Write _T_ (true) or _F_ (false).**

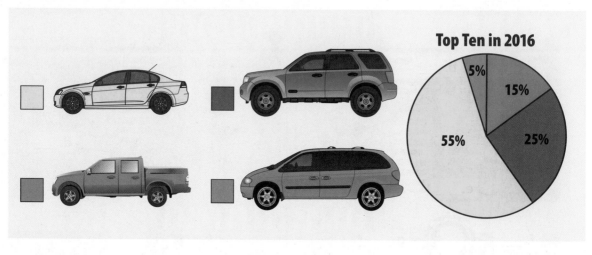

Top Ten in 2016

5%   15%   25%   55%

a. All of the cars are hybrids.   _F_

b. Fifteen percent are pickup trucks   ___

c. Twenty-five percent are SUVs.   ___

d. Twenty percent are tow trucks.   ___

e. Fifty-five percent are electric vehicles.   ___

f. Five percent are minivans.   ___

CHALLENGE   What do you think is the favorite color for cars in the U.S. this year?

160

**1. Check (✓) the things you do before you buy a used car.
Look in your dictionary for help.**

Word List: Buying and Maintaining a Car

☐ **Look at** car ads. ☐ **Negotiate** a price. ☐ **Fill** the tank with gas.

☐ **Ask** the seller about the car. ☐ **Get** the title from the seller. ☐ **Check** the oil.

☐ **Take** the car to a mechanic. ☐ **Register** the car. ☐ **Go** for a smog and safety check.

2. Unscramble the sentences.

a. car ads. at Look   *Look at car ads.*

b. oil. Check the   _____

c. car. the about Ask seller the   _____

d. gas. tank with Fill the   _____

e. Take a mechanic. car the to   _____

3. Look at the story. Put the sentences in order (1–6).

1.

2.

3.

4.

5.

6.

____ He registers his car.

_1_ Eduardo is looking at a car. He asks the seller some questions.

____ He fills the tank with gas.

____ Eduardo negotiates a good price.

____ He goes for a smog and safety check.

____ He gets the title from the seller.

Parts of a Car

1. Check (✓) the parts of a car that open. Look in your dictionary for help.

Word List: Parts of a Car

☐ windshield   ☐ tire   ☐ gas tank

☐ windshield wipers   ☐ headlight   ☐ trunk

☐ hood   ☐ bumper   ☐ engine

2. Read the sentences. Circle the correct words.

   a. The engine is under the (hood) / trunk.

   b. A car has four <u>tires</u> / <u>bumpers</u>.

   c. Use your <u>gas tank</u> / <u>headlights</u> at night.

   d. Use your <u>windshield wipers</u> / <u>windshield</u> in the rain.

   e. A car has two <u>engines</u> / <u>bumpers</u>.

   f. The <u>hood</u> / <u>trunk</u> is in the back of the car.

3. Label the picture. Use the words in the box.

hood	tire	~~windshield~~	bumper	headlight	wipers

a. <u>windshield</u>

b. _____

c. _____

d. _____

e. _____

f. _____

162

4. Check (✓) the things that only a driver uses. Look in your dictionary for help.

Word List: Parts of a Car		
☐ steering wheel	☐ audio display	☐ handbreak
☐ horn	☐ temperature control dial	☐ front seat
☐ turn signal	☐ fan speed	☐ seat belt
☐ rearview mirror	☐ AC button	☐ back seat

5. Match the words.

_2_ **a.** front   **1.** speed

___ **b.** fan   **2.** seat

___ **c.** temperature   **3.** display

___ **d.** audio   **4.** control dial

___ **e.** hand   **5.** mirror

___ **f.** rearview   **6.** brake

6. Complete the sentences. Use the words in the box.

| front seat | back seat | wheel | AC button | seat belt | horn | ~~turn signal~~ |

a. Use the _____ *turn signal* _____ before you turn.

b. Use the _____ to get attention.

c. Use the steering _____ to steer the car.

d. The driver sits in the _____ .

e. Always wear your _____ .

f. A baby is safe in the _____ .

g. Push the _____ on hot days.

163

 **An Airport**

1. Check (✓) the words you know. Look in your dictionary. Find the words you don't know.

Word List: An Airport

- ☐ ticket agent
- ☐ TSA agent
- ☐ gate
- ☐ flight attendant
- ☐ overhead compartment
- ☐ emergency exit
- ☐ passenger
- ☐ luggage
- ☐ e-ticket

- ☐ mobile boarding pass
- ☐ **Check in.**
- ☐ **Check** your bags.
- ☐ **Go through** security.
- ☐ **Board** the plane.
- ☐ **Put** your cell phone in airplane mode.
- ☐ **Take off.**
- ☐ **Land.**

2. Unscramble the sentences.

a. your here. Check bags   _Check your bags here._

b. plane. the Board   _____

c. plane The taking off. is   _____

d. at The plane 3:00. lands   _____

e. need to We check in.   _____

f. go security. through passengers All   _____

g. cell phone mode. your airplane in Put   _____

3. Match the words with the definitions.

_2_ **a.** flight attendant		**1.** a ticket you buy on the Internet
___ **b.** ticket agent		**2.** ~~person who works on an airplane~~
___ **c.** overhead compartment		**3.** someone who works at airport security
___ **d.** e-ticket		**4.** someone who sells tickets
___ **e.** gate		**5.** a place to put your luggage
___ **f.** TSA agent		**6.** you board the plane here

4. Look at the pictures. Circle the correct words.

a. Gloria is at the (airport) / emergency exit.

b. She has an e-ticket / airplane.

c. She doesn't need a boarding pass / ticket agent.

d. She's checking in / going through security at a computer.

e. She's going through security / boarding the plane.

f. The flight attendant / TSA agent is checking her boarding pass.

g. She's putting her luggage in the emergency exit / overhead compartment.

h. She's listening to the passenger / flight attendant.

i. Soon the airplane will land / take off.

5. How much do you like these jobs? Number the jobs 1–3 (1 = the job you like the best).

___ ticket agent

___ TSA agent

___ flight attendant

165

A Road Trip

1. Check (✓) the words you know. Look in your dictionary. Find the words you don't know.

Word List: A Road Trip

☐ wildlife   ☐ destination   ☐ **get** a ticket

☐ stars   ☐ **pack**   ☐ **run out** of gas

☐ scenery   ☐ **be** lost   ☐ **break down**

☐ automobile club card   ☐ **have** a flat tire

2. Match the words with the pictures.

1.

2.

3.

4.

5.

6.

7.

8.

9.

_4_ **a.** wildlife   ___ **d.** flat tire   ___ **g.** run out of gas

___ **b.** scenery   ___ **e.** break down   ___ **h.** be lost

___ **c.** automobile club card   ___ **f.** get a ticket   ___ **i.** pack

3. Look at the pictures. Circle the correct words.

a. Paul and Sara are taking a road (trip) / car.

b. Their wildlife / destination is Yellowstone National Park.

c. First, they pack / break down.

d. Paul drives carefully. He doesn't want a wildlife / ticket.

e. On the second day of the trip, the car gets a flat tire / ticket.

f. Paul calls the number on his automobile club card / destination.

g. They finally arrive in Yellowstone. The scenery / gas is beautiful.

h. They see many kinds of tickets / wildlife in the park.

i. At night, the sky is full of stars / scenery.

4. What about you? Answer the questions. Write *Yes, I do* or *No, I don't*.

a. Do you like to take road trips? _____ .

b. Do you have an automobile club card? _____ .

c. Do you usually pack too many things when you take a trip? _____ .

Job Search

1. Check (✓) the ways you find a job. Look in your dictionary for help.

> ### Word List: Job Search
>
> ☐ **set** a goal ☐ **look** for help wanted signs
>
> ☐ **write** a resume ☐ **check** employment websites
>
> ☐ **contact** references ☐ **complete** an application
>
> ☐ **talk** to friends ☐ **go on** an interview
>
> ☐ **go** to an employment agency ☐ **get** a job

2. Match the words.

_1_ **a.** get   **1.** a job

___ **b.** set a   **2.** references

___ **c.** write a   **3.** interview

___ **d.** complete an   **4.** goal

___ **e.** go on an   **5.** resume

___ **f.** contact   **6.** application

3. Study the chart. Complete the sentences. Use the words in the box.

> agency   talk   employment   help wanted   ~~check~~

a. Sixty percent ___check___ employment websites.

b. Thirty percent _____ to friends and family.

c. Five percent look for _____ signs.

d. Five percent go to an employment _____.

e. Forty percent don't check _____ websites.

How 100 Students Look for a Job

- 30%
- 60%
- 5%
- 5%

- ■ friends and family
- ■ employment agency
- ■ help wanted signs
- ■ employment websites

4. Check (✓) the things you can do on a computer.

- ✓ complete an application
- ☐ go on an interview
- ☐ write a resume
- ☐ check employment websites
- ☐ talk to friends
- ☐ look for help wanted signs

5. Look at the pictures. Then put the sentences in order (1–6).

1.
2.
3.
4.
5.
6.

- __3__ **a.** She looks for help wanted signs.
- ____ **b.** She talks to friends.
- ____ **c.** She gets a job.
- ____ **d.** She completes an application.
- ____ **e.** She writes a resume.
- ____ **f.** She goes on an interview.

1. Check (✓) the jobs you can do. Look in your dictionary for help.

Word List: Jobs and Occupations A–C

☐ accountant ☐ babysitter ☐ cashier

☐ assembler ☐ business owner ☐ childcare worker

☐ auto mechanic ☐ businessperson

2. Complete the words. Write the letters.

a. b _a_ bys _i_ t _t_ e r

b. bu __ i n e s __ p __ __ s __ n

c. __ s s e m __ l __ r

d. a __ __ o u n __ an __

e. __ a s __ i __ __

3. Look at the pictures. Circle the correct words.

a. She's a cashier / ~~childcare worker.~~

b. She's an <u>auto mechanic</u> / <u>assembler</u>.

c. He's a <u>babysitter</u> / <u>businessperson</u>.

d. He's a <u>business owner</u> / <u>accountant</u>.

e. She's an <u>accountant</u> / <u>assembler</u>.

f. He's a <u>babysitter</u> / <u>cashier</u>.

1. Check (✓) the jobs that are interesting to you. Look in your dictionary for help.

<table>
<tr><td colspan="3">Word List: Jobs and Occupations C–H</td></tr>
<tr><td>☐ computer technician</td><td>☐ firefighter</td><td>☐ garment worker</td></tr>
<tr><td>☐ delivery person</td><td>☐ florist</td><td>☐ hairdresser</td></tr>
<tr><td>☐ dental assistant</td><td>☐ gardener</td><td>☐ home healthcare aide</td></tr>
</table>

2. Match the words with the pictures.

1. 2. 3. 4. 5.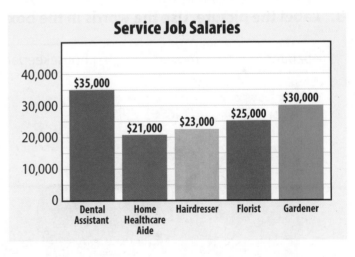

_4_ **a.** firefighter   ___ **c.** computer technician   ___ **e.** garment worker

___ **b.** hairdresser   ___ **d.** delivery person

3. Study the graph. Write the job names in order of salaries (highest to lowest).

a. _dental assistant_

b. _____

c. _____

d. _____

e. _____

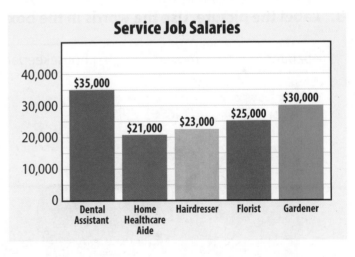

Service Job Salaries

Dental Assistant $35,000; Home Healthcare Aide $21,000; Hairdresser $23,000; Florist $25,000; Gardener $30,000

CHALLENGE Think about the jobs and the salaries in Exercise 3. Name the jobs you like. Write the jobs in order (1 = your favorite job).

1. Check (✓) three jobs people can do in a home. Look in your dictionary for help.

Word List: Jobs and Occupations H–P		
☐ homemaker	☐ manicurist	☐ musician
☐ housekeeper	☐ messenger	☐ nurse
☐ machine operator	☐ mover	☐ painter

2. Unscramble the words.

a. hemokamer   h _o_ _m_ e _m_ a _k_ er

b. runse   n __ __ __ e

c. iamcniruts   m __ n i c __ r __ __ t

d. peintar   __ a i __ __ __ r

e. engmesser   __ e __ __ e n __ __ __

f. inmhace ratorpeo   m a __ __ i n __   o p __ r __ t __ r

3. Label the picture. Use the words in the box.

painter	mover	housekeeper	musician	~~nurse~~

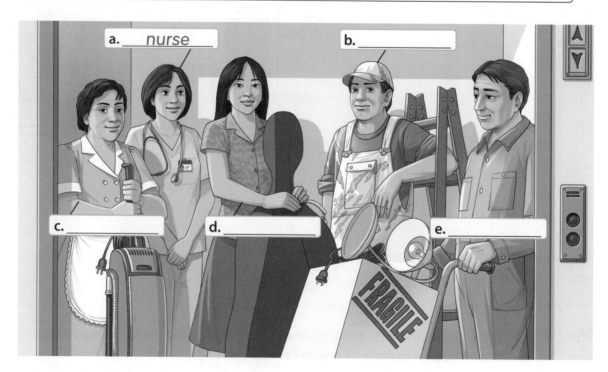

a. _nurse_   b. _____

c. _____   d. _____   e. _____

1. Check (✓) the jobs you don't need a college diploma for. Look in your dictionary for help.

Word List: Jobs and Occupations P–W

☐ postal worker ☐ security guard ☐ truck driver
☐ receptionist ☐ social worker ☐ veterinarian
☐ retail clerk ☐ stock clerk ☐ welder

2. Match the words with the sentences.

_5_ **a.** postal worker
___ **b.** social worker
___ **c.** retail clerk
___ **d.** security guard
___ **e.** receptionist
___ **f.** welder

1. I help families and children.
2. I can fix machines, pipes, and cars.
3. I answer phones and greet people.
4. I work in a clothing store.
5. I work at the post office.
6. I work in a bank.

3. Look at the pictures. Read the sentences. Number the people.

_4_ **a.**
b.
c.
d.
e.
f.

1. Sam's a security guard.
2. Francisco's a retail clerk.
3. Maria's a veterinarian.
4. Kima's a postal worker.
5. Don's a truck driver.
6. Samir's a stock clerk.

1. Check (✓) the things you do to plan for a career. Look in your dictionary for help.

Word List: Career Planning

- ☐ **visit** a career planning center
- ☐ **explore** career options
- ☐ **take** an interest inventory
- ☐ **list** your soft skills

- ☐ **set** a long-term goal
- ☐ **set** a short-term goal
- ☐ **attend** a job fair
- ☐ **speak** with a recruiter

2. Read the story. Circle the correct words.

a. Ahmed wants to ⟨explore⟩ / set his career options.

b. He lists / visits a career planning center.

c. At the center, he attends / takes an interest inventory.

d. He also lists / explores his soft skills.

e. Now, Ahmed sets / visits a short-term goal: He wants to take classes at City College.

f. He also sets a long-term skill / goal: He wants to be a software engineer.

g. He takes / attends a job fair.

h. At the fair, he speaks / visits with a recruiter. Ahmed has a job interview!

3. **Check (✓) the words you know. Look in your dictionary. Find the words you don't know.**

Word List: Career Planning

Career Path

☐ entry-level job   ☐ college degree

☐ training   ☐ promotion

☐ new job

Types of Training

☐ vocational training

☐ internship

☐ on-the-job training

☐ online course

---

4. **Unscramble the sentences.**

a. *It's an entry-level job.*

     an   It's   job.   entry-level

d. _____

     an   course.   online   It's

b. _____

     wants   Elda   promotion.   a

e. _____

     on-the-job   There's   training.

c. _____

     a   need   degree.   college   I

5. **Read the ads. Check (✓) the correct ad.**

1.

SALESPERSON WANTED
Entry level. Train on the job.
Call Marty at
555-3692

2.
BROADCAST HELP
Internship at TV station.
Promotion possible. Evenings
and weekends.
Apply at 254 South Street.

3.
JOBS! JOBS! JOBS!
Center St. Job Fair Sunday 8-4.
• Visit 40 companies
• Get information about
vocational training

	Ad #1	Ad #2	Ad #3
a. There is on-the-job training at this job.	✓	☐	☐
b. This ad is for an internship.	☐	☐	☐
c. You can learn about vocational training here.	☐	☐	☐
d. You can get a promotion at this job.	☐	☐	☐
e. This is a beginning level job.	☐	☐	☐

1. Check (✓) the things that are difficult to do. Look in your dictionary for help.

Word List: Job Skills		
☐ **do** manual labor	☐ **repair** appliances	☐ **supervise** people
☐ **drive** a truck	☐ **sell** cars	☐ **take care of** children
☐ **program** computers	☐ **sew** clothes	☐ **use** a cash register

2. Match the words with the pictures.

1.

2.

3.

4.

5.

6.

_2_ **a.** program computers   ___ **c.** repair appliances   ___ **e.** do manual labor

___ **b.** use a cash register   ___ **d.** supervise people   ___ **f.** sell cars

3. Complete the sentences. Use the words in the box.

use a cash register	~~drive a truck~~	sew clothes
take care of children	do manual labor	

a. Deon is a truck driver. He can _drive a truck_.

b. Karen is a childcare worker. She can _____.

c. Maya is a cashier. She can _____.

d. Adan is a garment worker. He can _____.

e. Dishi is a gardener. He can _____.

1. Check (✓) the things you can do. Look in your dictionary for help.

Word List: Office Skills

☐ **type** a letter	☐ **staple**	☐ **leave** a message
☐ **enter** data	☐ **fax** a document	☐ **take** a message
☐ **make** copies	☐ **print** a document	☐ **check** messages

2. Write the words in the chart. Use the words in the box.

take a message	enter data	type a letter	leave a message
make copies	~~check messages~~	staple	

On the Phone	At the Copy Machine	At the Computer
a. *check messages*	d.	f.
b.	e.	g.
c.		

3. Look at the pictures. Put the sentences in order (1–5).

1.

2.

3.

4.

5.

____ He prints the letter.

____ He faxes the letter.

____ He makes copies of the letter.

____ He puts the copies on his supervisor's desk.

_1_ Santiago is typing a letter for his supervisor.

⎡CHALLENGE⎤ Think about Santiago's office skills. Name four things he can do.

177

Soft Skills

1. **Check (✓) the words you know. Look in your dictionary. Find the words you don't know.**

Word List: Soft Skills		
☐ **solve** problems	☐ **communicate** clearly	☐ patient
☐ **make** decisions	☐ **cooperate** with teammates	☐ willing to learn
☐ **manage** time	☐ **respond** well to feedback	☐ honest

2. **Look at the pictures. Circle the correct words.**

a. Antonia teaches small children.
   She is very (patient) / honest.

Thanks. I can fix that.

b. Mark listens to the boss.
   He responds well to decisions / feedback.

c. Koji doesn't take the money. It's not his money, and he is willing to learn / honest.

d. Anya is a good employee. She cooperates clearly / with her teammates.

3. **What about you? Check (✓) your answers.**

Are you…?
☐ patient
☐ honest
☐ willing to learn

Can you…?
☐ solve problems
☐ manage time
☐ make decisions

Do you…?
☐ cooperate with teammates
☐ respond well to feedback
☐ communicate clearly

1. Check (✓) the things to do before an interview. Look in your dictionary for help.

Word List: Interview Skills

☐ **Prepare** for the interview. ☐ **Don't be** late. ☐ **Listen** carefully.

☐ **Be** neat. ☐ **Turn off** your cell phone. ☐ **Ask** questions.

☐ **Bring** your resume and ID. ☐ **Shake** hands. ☐ **Write** a thank-you note.

2. Match the words with the pictures.

1.

2.

3.

4.

5.

<u>4</u> **a.** Turn off your cell phone. ___ **c.** Write a thank-you note. ___ **e.** Don't be late.

___ **b.** Shake hands. ___ **d.** Bring your ID.

3. Complete the crossword puzzle.

Across

1. ___ for the interview.

3. ___ carefully.

5. ___ questions.

Down

2. Bring your ___.

3. Don't be ___.

4. Be ___.

	¹P	²R	E	P	A	R	E
3					4		
					5		

First Day on the Job

1. Check (✓) the words you know. Look in your dictionary. Find the words you don't know.

> ### Word List: First Day on the Job
>
> ☐ facility   ☐ co-worker   ☐ **direct**
>
> ☐ staff   ☐ shift   ☐ **distribute**
>
> ☐ team player   ☐ **yell**
>
> ☐ resident   ☐ **complain**

2. Complete the sentences. Use the words in the box.

> co-worker   staff   direct   yell   ~~distribute~~   shift

a. Can you ___distribute___ these for me, please? One to each employee.

b. You don't need to _____. I can hear you!

c. This is the end of his _____. He's going home now.

d. I'm lost. Can you _____ me to the office?

e. Alicia works hard. She's a great _____.

f. We have a large _____. There are over 100 employees here.

180

3. Read the story. Circle the correct words.

a. Clara works at a nursing home (facility)/ shift.

b. There are five people on the resident / staff.

c. Clara helps her co-workers / facility.

d. She is a resident / team player.

e. A few of the residents / staff are over 90 years old.

f. Sometimes they are not happy and they distribute / complain.

g. Clara's shift / facility begins at 1:00 p.m.

h. At 2:00 p.m. she directs / distributes juice and water to the residents.

4. What about you? Answer the questions.

a. When does your shift begin? _____ When does it end? _____

b. How many co-workers do you have? _____

c. What does a team player do? _____

d. Are you a team player? _____

The Workplace

1. Check (✓) the words for people. Look in your dictionary for help.

Word List: The Workplace		
☐ entrance	☐ safety regulations	☐ pay stub
☐ customer	☐ time clock	☐ wages
☐ office	☐ supervisor	☐ deductions
☐ employer / boss	☐ employee	☐ paycheck
☐ receptionist	☐ payroll clerk	

2. Match the words with the pictures.

1.

2.

3.

4.

5.

___3___ **a.** employee   ____ **c.** payroll clerk   ____ **e.** employer

____ **b.** receptionist   ____ **d.** supervisor

3. Read the sentences. Circle the correct words.

a. Customers use the (entrance) / time clock.

b. A receptionist works in the deductions / office.

c. The employees use the time clock / payroll.

d. The payroll clerk works with safety regulations / paychecks.

e. It's important for employees to have safety regulations / receptionists.

f. A pay stub shows the employee's boss / wages and deductions.

4. Label the picture. Write the numbers.

1. time clock
2. supervisor
3. employee entrance
4. safety regulations
5. ~~employee~~

a. 5

5. Study the pay stub. Write *T* (true) or *F* (false).

Pay Period: 08 07 2017 to 08 18 2017
Employee Name: Ronald Jenkins
Employee Number: 24592

Earnings		Deductions			
Total Wages	$240.00	**Taxes**		**Net Pay** (paycheck amount)	$208.06
		Federal	$12.50		
		Medicare	$ 3.45		
		State	$ 1.44		
		Social Security	$14.55		

a. The employer's first name is Ronald. ___F___ d. Ron's deductions are $240.00. ____

b. The payroll clerk's name is Net. ____ e. There are four kinds of deductions. ____

c. The employee's last name is Jenkins. ____ f. The total wages are $208.06. ____

[CHALLENGE] Look at the taxes on the pay stub. What is the total?

Inside a Company

1. Check (✓) the words you know. Look in your dictionary. Find the words you don't know.

> ### Word List: Inside a Company
>
> ☐ headquarters   ☐ sales   ☐ customer service
>
> ☐ warehouse   ☐ accounting   ☐ building maintenance
>
> ☐ research and development   ☐ information technology   ☐ security

2. Match the words with the pictures.

1.

2.

3.

4.

5.

6.

_3_ **a.** information technology   ___ **d.** headquarters

___ **b.** security   ___ **e.** warehouse

___ **c.** building maintenance   ___ **f.** customer service

3. Complete the sentences. Use the words in the box.

> research   accounting   sales   maintenance   ~~customer~~

a. Alan talks on the phone all day. He works in _customer_ service.

b. Mia is a scientist. She works in _____ and development.

c. Pedro sells computers. He works in the _____ department.

d. Fadia is good at math. She works in the _____ department.

e. Bo fixes things. He works in building _____.

1. Check (✓) the words you know. Look in your dictionary. Find the words you don't know.

Word List: Manufacturing		
☐ factory owner	☐ assembly line	☐ forklift
☐ factory worker	☐ warehouse	☐ shipping clerk
☐ parts	☐ conveyor belt	☐ loading dock

2. Complete the chart. Use all the words in the Word List.

Places at Work	Things at Work	People at Work
a. *assembly line*	d.	g.
b.	e.	h.
c.	f.	i.

3. Label the picture. Use the words in the box.

| factory worker | factory owner | assembly line | conveyor belt | parts | ~~factory~~ |

a. *factory*

b. _____

c. _____

d. _____

e. _____

f. _____

CHALLENGE Name three things from the Word List that are NOT in the picture.

Landscaping and Gardening

1. **Check (✓) the words you know. Look in your dictionary. Find the words you don't know.**

Word List: Landscaping and Gardening		
☐ leaf blower	☐ rake	☐ **trim** the hedges
☐ lawn mower	☐ hedge clippers	☐ **rake** the leaves
☐ shovel	☐ **mow** the lawn	☐ **plant** a tree

2. **Match the words with the pictures.**

1.

2.

3.

4.

5.

_5_ **a.** leaf blower   ___ **c.** lawn mower   ___ **e.** hedge clippers

___ **b.** rake   ___ **d.** shovel

3. **Look at the pictures. Complete the sentences.**

a. Tim will mow the lawn for ___$12.00___.

b. Tim will plant a tree for _____.

c. Tim will trim the hedges for _____.

d. Tim will rake the leaves and plant a tree for _____.

e. Tim will mow the lawn, trim the hedges, and rake the leaves for _____.

1. **Check (✓) the things that grow on a farm. Look in your dictionary for help.**

<table>
<tr><td colspan="3">**Word List: Farming and Ranching**</td></tr>
<tr><td>☐ rice</td><td>☐ field</td><td>☐ hay</td></tr>
<tr><td>☐ wheat</td><td>☐ barn</td><td>☐ rancher</td></tr>
<tr><td>☐ soybeans</td><td>☐ farmer</td><td></td></tr>
<tr><td>☐ corn</td><td>☐ livestock</td><td></td></tr>
</table>

2. **Write the words in the chart. Use the words in the box.**

rice	farmer	~~field~~	barn	rancher	soybeans	wheat

	Places		People		Plants
a.	*field*	c.		e.	
b.		d.		f.	
				g.	

3. **Look at the picture. Write T (true) or F (false).**

a. The farmer is in the barn. ___T___

b. The farmer has livestock. _____

c. The farmer is putting corn on the truck. _____

d. The hay is in the truck. _____

e. The truck is in the field. _____

f. There are soybeans on the truck. _____

Office Work

1. Check (✓) the words you know. Look in your dictionary. Find the words you don't know.

Word List: Office Work

☐ supply cabinet ☐ office manager ☐ computer technician
☐ conference room ☐ file clerk ☐ reception area
☐ cubicle ☐ file cabinet

2. Complete the chart. Use all the words in the Word List.

People	Places	Things
a. *office manager*	d.	g.
b.	e.	h.
c.	f.	

3. Complete the sentences. Circle the correct words.

a. Maria is in the conference room / reception area.

b. She's a file clerk / receptionist.

c. Zahra is the office manager / receptionist.

d. She's in the file / conference room.

e. Victor is a computer technician / file clerk.

f. He's putting files in the reception area / file cabinet.

g. Linda is an office manager / a computer technician.

h. She's fixing a computer in a cubicle / conference room.

4. Check (✓) the things you use at home or at work. Look in your dictionary for help.

> ### Word List: Office Work
>
> **Office Equipment**
> ☐ computer
> ☐ printer
> ☐ scanner
> ☐ fax machine
> ☐ photocopier
>
> **Office Supplies**
> ☐ stapler
> ☐ staples
> ☐ paper clip
> ☐ glue

5. Unscramble the words.

a. spatles   s _t_ a _p_ _l_ e _s_

b. leug   g __ u __

c. rentpri   p __ i __ t e __

d. nerscan   s __ __ n n __ __

e. cupemtor   __ o m __ u __ e __

f. eppar plic   __ __ p e__   __ l i

6. Label the picture. Use the words in the box.

| computer | fax machine | glue | paper clips | stapler | printer | ~~photocopier~~ |

a. _photocopier_

b. _____

c. _____

d. _____

e. _____

f. _____

g. _____

Information Technology (IT)

1. Check (✓) the things that are on your desk. Look in your dictionary for help.

Word List: Information Technology (IT)		
☐ monitor	☐ mouse	☐ laptop computer
☐ desktop computer	☐ hard drive	☐ keyboard
☐ power cord	☐ printer	☐ speaker

2. Match the words with the sentences.

_5_ **a.** monitor

____ **b.** keyboard

____ **c.** speaker

____ **d.** printer

____ **e.** hard drive

1. Use this to type.

2. The computer keeps information here.

3. Listen to music on this.

4. Use this to print documents.

5. ~~Watch videos on this.~~

3. Label the picture. Use the words in the box.

~~monitor~~	desktop computer	laptop	keyboard	mouse	power cord

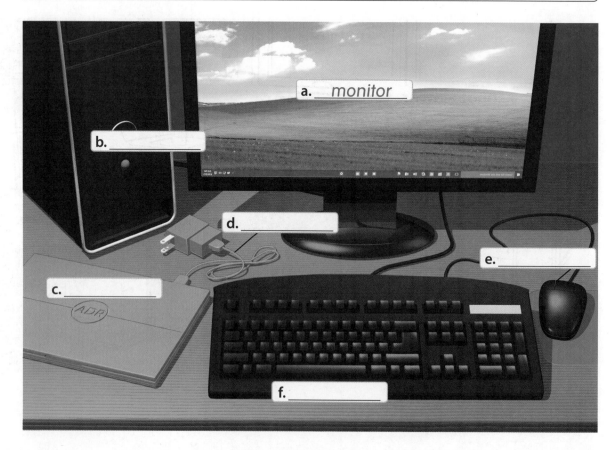

a. _monitor_

b. _____

c. _____

d. _____

e. _____

f. _____

4. Check (✓) the words you know. Look in your dictionary. Find the words you don't know.

Word List: Information Technology (IT)		
☐ Wi-Fi connection	☐ mic	☐ The screen **froze**.
☐ modem	☐ webcam	☐ It **won't print**.
☐ headset	☐ The computer **won't start**.	☐ I **can't stream** video.

5. Match the words with the pictures.

1.  2.  3.  4. 5.

_3_ **a.** headset   ___ **c.** modem   ___ **e.** Wi-Fi connection

___ **b.** mic   ___ **d.** webcam

6. Complete the sentences. Use the words in the box.

Wi-Fi	~~start~~	print	stream	froze

a. The computer won't _____start_____. The screen is black.

b. I can't type. The screen _____.

c. There's a problem with the printer. It won't _____.

d. I have a bad _____ connection. I can't _____ video.

CHALLENGE   Look at a computer near you. Write the names of things you see.

1. **Check (✓) the hotel jobs. Look in your dictionary for help.**

<table>
<tr><td colspan="3">Word List: A Hotel</td></tr>
<tr><td>☐ doorman</td><td>☐ luggage cart</td><td>☐ guest room</td></tr>
<tr><td>☐ parking attendant</td><td>☐ desk clerk</td><td>☐ room service</td></tr>
<tr><td>☐ bellhop</td><td>☐ front desk</td><td>☐ housekeeper</td></tr>
</table>

2. **Match the words.**

_5_ **a.** guest   **1.** cart

___ **b.** luggage   **2.** clerk

___ **c.** room   **3.** attendant

___ **d.** front   **4.** desk

___ **e.** desk   **5.** ~~room~~

___ **f.** parking   **6.** service

3. **Look at the picture. Read the sentences. Number the people.**

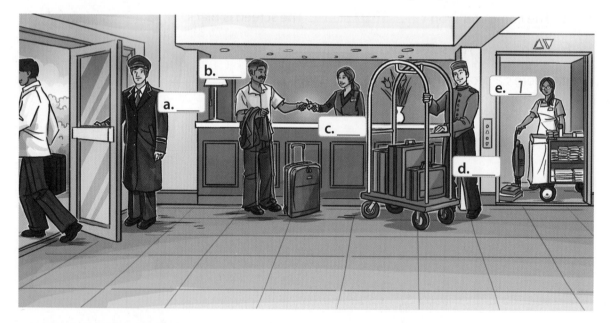

1. ~~Leela is a housekeeper.~~   4. Ken is a bellhop.

2. Elena is a desk clerk.   5. Ron is a doorman.

3. Amal is a guest at the hotel.

1. Check (✓) the food service jobs. Look in your dictionary for help.

Word List: Food Service

☐ short-order cook   ☐ storeroom   ☐ diner

☐ dishwasher   ☐ head chef   ☐ buffet

☐ walk-in freezer   ☐ server   ☐ headwaiter

2. Unscramble the sentences.

a. in The dishwasher the is kitchen.   _The dishwasher is in the kitchen._

b. servers food. the bring The   _____

c. at The diners the buffet. are   _____

d. There's in meat walk-in freezer. the   _____

e. in The storeroom. short-order cook is the   _____

3. What's wrong with the picture? Circle the correct words.

a. The (diner)/ head chef is washing dishes.

b. The diner / dishwasher is eating.

c. The head chef is sleeping in the storeroom / freezer.

d. The cook / headwaiter is eating the soup.

e. The walk-in freezer / buffet is open.

Tools and Building Supplies

1. Check (✓) the things you have at home. Look in your dictionary for help.

Word List: Tools and Building Supplies		
☐ hammer	☐ 2 x 4 (two by four)	☐ screw
☐ handsaw	☐ paintbrush	☐ nail
☐ electric drill	☐ paint roller	☐ tape measure
☐ extension cord	☐ paint	☐ duct tape
☐ pipe	☐ screwdriver	☐ sandpaper

2. Cross out the word that doesn't belong.

a. ~~paint roller~~   extension cord   electric drill

b. paint   duct tape   paintbrush

c. sandpaper   screw   nail

d. screwdriver   screw   2 x 4

e. hammer   pipe   nail

3. Read the labels. Draw the pictures.

a. paintbrush

b. screwdriver

c. hammer

d. duct tape

e. nail

f. tape measure

4. Answer the questions. Use the words in the box.

a handsaw	a nail	a hammer	a paintbrush	~~a tape measure~~
2 x 4s	paint	a drill	a paint roller	screws

a. What does John need?

a tape measure

_____

_____

b. What does Irene need?

_____

_____

_____

c. What does Ron need?

_____

_____

_____

_____

5. What about you? Answer the questions.

a. What tools and supplies do you have? _____

b. Where do you buy tools and supplies? _____

c. Where do you keep your tools and supplies? _____

CHALLENGE Name three tools and supplies that are expensive. Name three that are cheap. Make a list.

Construction

1. **Check (✓) the words you know. Look in your dictionary.
   Find the words you don't know.**

Word List: Construction		
☐ construction worker	☐ tile	☐ **paint**
☐ ladder	☐ bricks	☐ **lay** bricks
☐ concrete	☐ wood	☐ **install** tile

2. **Complete the words. Write the letters.**

   a. w _o_ _o_ d

   b. l a __ __ e __

   c. t __ __ e

   d. b __ __ c __ s

   e. __ o n c __ __ __ e

   f. c o __ s t __ __ c __ i o __   w __ __ __ e r

3. **Look at the picture. Read the sentences. Number the people.**

1. Mario is installing tile.
2. Ben has a ladder.
3. Tisha is painting.

4. Ali is laying bricks.
5. ~~Max is working with concrete.~~
6. Luis is getting more bricks.

1. Check (✓) the things that are not safe. Look in your dictionary for help.

Word List: Job Safety

☐ careless worker   ☐ slippery floor   ☐ knee pads

☐ careful worker   ☐ safety goggles   ☐ safety boots

☐ broken equipment   ☐ earplugs   ☐ fire extinguisher

2. Match the words with the sentences.

_5_ **a.** broken equipment

___ **b.** fire extinguisher

___ **c.** slippery floor

___ **d.** safety goggles

___ **e.** safety boots

___ **f.** knee pads

1. It protects you from fire.

2. They protect your knees.

3. They protect your eyes.

4. They protect your feet.

5. ~~It's not safe to use this at work.~~

6. It's not safe to walk here.

3. Look at the pictures. Check (✓) the correct sentences.

a. ☑ He's using his earplugs.

☐ He's using broken equipment.

b. ☐ She's wearing safety boots.

☐ She's wearing knee pads.

c. ☐ He's careless.

☐ The floor is slippery.

d. ☐ The extinguisher is broken.

☐ He's a careful worker.

A Bad Day at Work

1. Check (✓) the words you know. Look in your dictionary. Find the words you don't know.

Word List: A Bad Day at Work		
☐ dangerous	☐ floor plan	☐ wiring
☐ clinic	☐ contractor	☐ bricklayer
☐ budget	☐ electrical hazard	☐ **call in** sick

2. Match the words with the pictures.

1.

2.
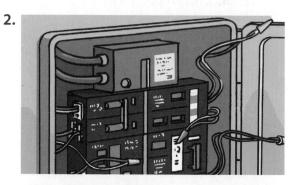

3.

4.

5.

6.

<u>5</u> **a.** contractor ___ **c.** clinic ___ **e.** wiring

___ **b.** bricklayer ___ **d.** electrical hazard ___ **f.** floor plan

198

3. Look at the pictures. Circle the correct words.

a. Sam is a good <u>customer</u> / <u>contractor</u>.

b. He and the customer are looking at the <u>floor plan</u> / <u>bricklayer</u>.

c. Next they will look at the <u>budget</u> / <u>bricklayer</u>.

d. Construction work can be <u>careful</u> / <u>dangerous</u>.

e. Sam always looks for electrical hazards and bad <u>budgets</u> / <u>wiring</u>.

f. Sam is having a <u>bad day</u> / <u>hazard</u> today. He hurt his back.

g. He's <u>dangerous</u> / <u>at the clinic</u>.

h. The doctor says he can't <u>wire</u> / <u>work</u> all week.

i. Poor Sam. He doesn't like to <u>be a contractor</u> / <u>call in sick</u>.

4. What about you? Answer the questions.

a. Do you have a dangerous job? _____

b. Do you know other people with dangerous jobs? _____

c. Name three jobs you think are dangerous. Use your dictionary for help.

_____ _____ _____

Schools and Subjects

1. Check (✓) the schools near your home. Look in your dictionary for help.

Word List: Schools and Subjects

☐ preschool   ☐ high school   ☐ college / university

☐ elementary school   ☐ vocational school   ☐ adult school

☐ middle school   ☐ community college

2. Label the schools. Use the words in the box.

preschool   elementary school   ~~high school~~   vocational school   adult school

a. ___high school___   b. _____   c. _____

d. _____   e. _____

3. Read the sentences. Circle the correct words.

a. Tina is seven years old. She goes to <u>preschool</u> / (<u>elementary school</u>).

b. Brandon is three. He goes to <u>preschool / vocational school</u>.

c. Mike studies electronics. He goes to <u>vocational /middle</u> school.

d. Sun is 16 years old. She goes to <u>middle / high</u> school.

e. Omar is in medical school. He goes to a <u>community college / university</u>.

f. Minh learns English at the community center. She goes to <u>middle / adult</u> school.

4. Check (✓) the subjects you like to study. Look in your dictionary for help.

Word List: Schools and Subjects		
☐ language arts	☐ history	☐ arts
☐ math	☐ world languages	☐ music
☐ science	☐ English language instruction	☐ physical education

5. Match the words with the pictures.

_3_ **a.** music

___ **b.** science

___ **c.** English language instruction

___ **d.** math

___ **e.** history

___ **f.** world languages

1.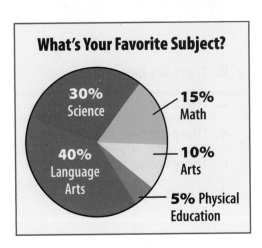

2.

3.

4.

5.

6.

6. Study the chart. Complete the sentences.

a. Forty percent of students like ___*language arts*___.

b. Ten percent of students like _____.

c. Forty-five percent of students like math and _____.

d. Five percent of students like _____.

What's Your Favorite Subject?

- 30% Science
- 15% Math
- 40% Language Arts
- 10% Arts
- 5% Physical Education

CHALLENGE What's your favorite subject? Ask three people. Write their answers.

English Composition

1. **Read "Say it with Flowers" on page 217. Check (✓) the things you see. Look in your dictionary for help.**

Word List: English Composition		
☐ word	☐ period	☐ comma
☐ sentence	☐ question mark	☐ quotation marks
☐ paragraph	☐ exclamation point	☐ apostrophe

2. **Follow the directions.**

   a. **Circle the period.**
      There's my book.

   b. **Circle the quotation marks.**
      "Be careful!"

   c. **Circle the word with an apostrophe.**
      Where is Tom's car?

   d. **Circle the question mark.**
      What's on your desk?

   e. **Circle the commas.**
      There's a desk, a chair, and a pencil.

   f. **Circle the exclamation point.**
      The police officer said, "Stop!"

3. **Read the paragraph. Circle the punctuation. Then write _T_ (true) or _F_ (false).**

   Today we are studying English composition. We're learning about sentences and punctuation. I know that sentences need a period, a question mark, or an exclamation mark. Some words need apostrophes. Do you know how to use quotation marks?

   a. There is one paragraph. ___T___

   b. There are eight sentences. ____

   c. There are two commas. ____

   d. There are two question marks. ____

   e. There is one apostrophe. ____

   f. There are 25 words. ____

4. Check (✓) the things you like to do. Look in your dictionary for help.

Word List: English Composition
☐ **Brainstorm** ideas.   ☐ **Write** a first draft.   ☐ **Rewrite.**   ☐ **Organize** your ideas.   ☐ **Edit.**   ☐ **Hand in** your paper.

5. Match the words with the pictures.

1.   2.   3.

4.   5.   6.

_1_ **a.** write   ___ **c.** hand in   ___ **e.** edit

___ **b.** brainstorm   ___ **d.** organize   ___ **f.** rewrite

6. Complete the sentences. Use the words in the box.

ideas	organize	~~composition~~	draft	rewrite	hand in

a. The students are writing a _composition_ .

b. They brainstorm _____ .

c. They _____ their ideas.

d. They write a first _____ .

e. They edit and _____ their work.

f. Then they _____ their papers.

Mathematics

1. **Check (✓) the words you know. Look in your dictionary. Find the words you don't know.**

Word List: Mathematics	
☐ negative integers	☐ add
☐ positive integers	☐ subtract
☐ odd numbers	☐ multiply
☐ even numbers	☐ divide

2. **Match the numbers with the words.**

_4_ **a.** 1, 3, 5   **1.** positive three

___ **b.** −3   **2.** even numbers

___ **c.** 2, 4, 6   **3.** negative three

___ **d.** 3   **4.** odd numbers

___ **e.** 10 + 2   **5.** add

___ **f.** 10 × 2   **6.** subtract

___ **g.** 10 ÷ 2   **7.** multiply

___ **h.** 10 − 2   **8.** divide

3. **Do the math. Then circle all the correct letters.**

a. $4 \times 4 =$ _16_

b. $2 - 6 =$ ___

c. $7 + 2 =$ ___

d. $9 \div 3 =$ ___

1. This problem has a negative answer.	a	ⓑ	c	d
2. This problem has no even numbers.	a	b	c	d
3. These problems have no odd numbers.	a	b	c	d
4. These problems have positive answers.	a	b	c	d

4. Check (✓) the lines, shapes, and angles you see in your classroom. Look in your dictionary for help.

Word List: Mathematics		
☐ straight line	☐ right angle	☐ triangle
☐ curved line	☐ rectangle	☐ circle
☐ parallel lines	☐ square	

5. Cross out the word that doesn't belong.

a. straight ~~right~~ curved

b. rectangle square circle

c. triangle square curved line

d. triangle circle curved line

e. right angle parallel lines straight line

6. Read the labels. Draw the pictures.

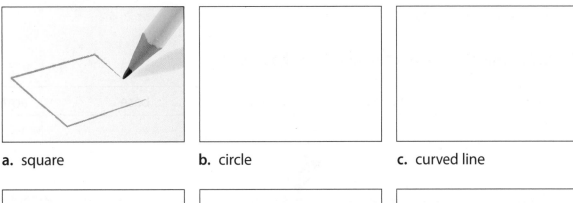

a. square   b. circle   c. curved line

d. parallel lines   e. triangle   f. rectangle

CHALLENGE How many lines are in a square? A triangle? A circle?

1. **Check (✓) the things a biologist can see with a microscope.
   Look in your dictionary for help.**

Word List: Science			
Biology		**Microscope**	
☐ organisms	☐ slide	☐ eyepiece	☐ base
☐ biologist	☐ cell	☐ stage	☐ arm
	☐ nucleus		

2. **Read the sentences. Circle the correct words.**

   a. A biologist studies (biology) / a base.

   b. All organisms have slides / cells.

   c. Every cell has a nucleus / an arm.

   d. A biologist uses a microscope / nucleus to see small organisms.

   e. Put the slide on the eyepiece / stage.

   f. Use the base / eyepiece to see the slide.

3. **Label the picture. Use the words in the box.**

stage	~~eyepiece~~	slide	base	arm

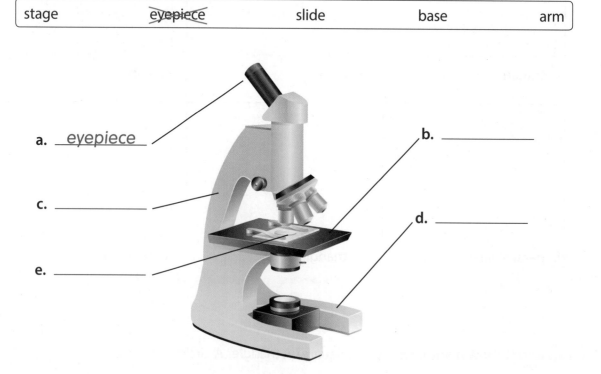

a. _eyepiece_

b. _____

c. _____

d. _____

e. _____

4. Check (✓) the things a chemist studies. Look in your dictionary for help.

Word List: Science	
Chemistry	**A Science Lab**

Chemistry

☐ chemist   ☐ molecule

☐ periodic table   ☐ atom

A Science Lab

☐ Bunsen burner   ☐ forceps

☐ beaker   ☐ dropper

☐ test tube

5. Unscramble the words.

a. karbee   b _e_ _a_ k _e_ _r_

b. sitmhec   c __ __ m __ __ t

c. preorpd   d __ __ p p __ __

d. mtao   __ __ __ m

e. focresp   __ o r __ __ p __

f. clueelom   m __ l __ c __ __ __

6. Look at the picture. Circle the correct words.

a. There are three test tubes / beakers.

b. The chemist / periodic table is reading.

c. The droppers / forceps are next to the Bunsen burner.

d. There are four test tubes / droppers.

e. The chemist is studying molecules / a Bunsen burner.

f. There's a molecule / periodic table on the wall.

207

1. Check (✓) the wars you know about. Look in your dictionary for help.

Word List: U.S. History		
☐ thirteen colonies	☐ Declaration of Independence	☐ Civil War
☐ colonists	☐ Revolutionary War	☐ World War I
☐ Native Americans	☐ Constitution	☐ World War II
	☐ Bill of Rights	

2. Take the test. Bubble in the answers.

Name: _____   Date: _____

1. Ⓐ ●Ⓑ Ⓒ Ⓓ   3. Ⓐ Ⓑ Ⓒ Ⓓ   5. Ⓐ Ⓑ Ⓒ Ⓓ
2. Ⓐ Ⓑ Ⓒ Ⓓ   4. Ⓐ Ⓑ Ⓒ Ⓓ   6. Ⓐ Ⓑ Ⓒ Ⓓ

1. Name the war between the thirteen colonies and England.

   a. the Civil War
   b. the Revolutionary War
   c. World War I
   d. World War II

2. Name the war between the states of the United States.

   a. the Civil War
   b. the Bill of Rights
   c. World War I
   d. the Revolutionary War

3. Name the document that has the laws of the United States.

   a. the Declaration of Independence
   b. the Constitution
   c. the Colonist
   d. the Thirteen Colonies

4. Name the first people to live in North America.

   a. revolutionaries
   b. Bill of Rights
   c. Native Americans
   d. colonists

5. Name the first people from Europe to live in North America.

   a. colonies
   b. colonists
   c. Native Americans
   d. revolutionaries

6. Name the war from 1941–1945.

   a. the Civil War
   b. the Revolutionary War
   c. World War I
   d. World War II

CHALLENGE   Name three rights in the Bill of Rights.

1. **Check (✓) the words for people. Look in your dictionary for help.**

Word List: World History

☐ exploration   ☐ army   ☐ inventor

☐ explorer   ☐ immigration   ☐ invention

☐ war   ☐ immigrant

2. **Complete the words. Write the letters.**

a. e _X_ p l _O_ r e _r_

b. a ___ ___ y

c. ___ ___ r

d. ___ n v ___ n t ___ ___ n

e. ___ m m ___ g ___ a ___ ___

f. e x ___ ___ o ___ a t ___ ___ ___

3. **Look at the pictures. Circle the correct words.**

a. Alexander Graham Bell was an (inventor) / explorer.

b. The telephone was an important invention / immigration.

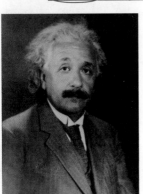

c. Albert Einstein was a famous army / immigrant. He came to the U.S. in 1933.

d. Marco Polo was an explorer / immigration officer. He went to China.

Digital Literacy

1. **Check (✓) the words you know. Look in your dictionary. Find the words you don't know.**

<table>
<tr><td colspan="3" align="center">Word List: Digital Literacy</td></tr>
<tr><td>☐ open the program</td><td>☐ close the document</td><td>☐ delete a word</td></tr>
<tr><td>☐ type</td><td>☐ quit the program</td><td>☐ copy text</td></tr>
<tr><td>☐ save the document</td><td>☐ click on the screen</td><td>☐ paste text</td></tr>
</table>

2. **Unscramble the words.**

   a. tqiu teh rompgra   q _u_ _i_ _t_ _t_ h _e_ pr _o_ _g_ _r_ _a_ _m_

   b. seva eth udocmnte   s _ _ _ _ the _ _ _ _ _ _ _ _ t

   c. ycpo ttxe   _ _ _ _ y _ _ e _ _ _

   d. ledete a owdr   _ e _ _ _ _ _ a _ _ _ _ d

   e. ptye   _ _ _ _

   f. licck no hte escnre   _ _ _ _ _ k _ _ _ t _ _ _ _ _ c _ _ _ _ _ _

3. **Label the pictures. Write the numbers.**

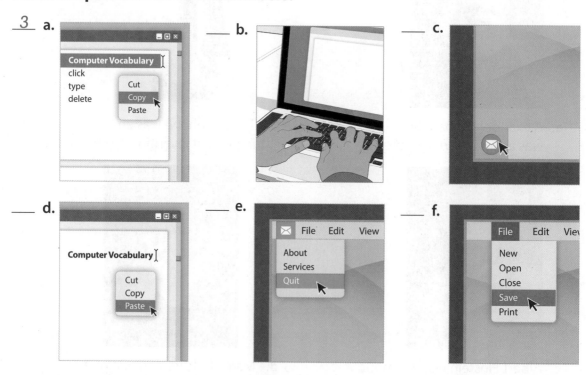

   _3_ **a.**   __ **b.**   __ **c.**

   __ **d.**   __ **e.**   __ **f.**

   1. Open the program.   **3.** ~~Copy text.~~   **5.** Save the document.

   2. Type.   **4.** Paste text.   **6.** Quit the program.

4. Check (✓) the things you always do when you send an email. Look in your dictionary for help.

Word List: Digital Literacy

☐ **type** the password   ☐ **type** the subject   ☐ **attach** a file

☐ **log in** to your account   ☐ **write** the message   ☐ **send** the email

☐ **address** the email   ☐ **check** your spelling

5. Look at the pictures. Circle the correct words.

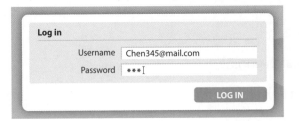

a. First, Chen types his <u>file / password</u>.

b. <u>He logs in to / addresses</u> his account.

c. Then he types the <u>subject / spelling</u> of the email.

d. He <u>addresses / checks</u> the email to his boss.

e. He <u>attaches / writes</u> his message.

f. Then he <u>types / attaches</u> a file.

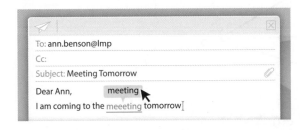

g. He <u>checks / types</u> his spelling.

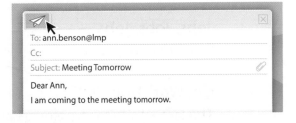

h. Finally, he <u>sends / logs in</u> the email.

211

Internet Research

1. **Check (✓) the things you use or do every day. Look in your dictionary for help.**

Word List: Internet Research		
☐ search engine	☐ links	☐ **look** at the results
☐ search box	☐ **select** a search engine	☐ **click** on a link
☐ search results	☐ **type** in a question	☐ **bookmark** a site

2. **Match the words.**

   _2_ **a.** select

   ___ **b.** type

   ___ **c.** look

   ___ **d.** click

   ___ **e.** bookmark

   1. a site

   2. ~~a search engine~~

   3. on a link

   4. in a question

   5. at the results

3. **Label the picture. Use the words in the box.**

links	search box	~~search engine~~	search results

212

4. Check (✓) the words you know. Look in your dictionary. Find the words you don't know.

Word List: Internet Research

- ☐ browser window
- ☐ menu bar
- ☐ back button
- ☐ URL
- ☐ refresh button
- ☐ web page
- ☐ tab
- ☐ drop-down menu
- ☐ video player

5. Label the picture. Use all of the words in the Word List.

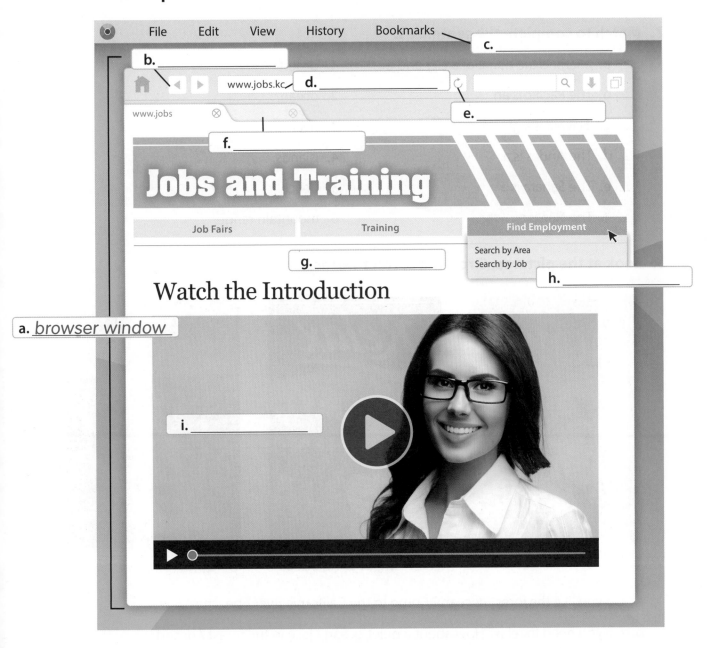

a. *browser window*

CHALLENGE   Open a browser window on your computer or phone. Name the things you see.

Geography and Habitats

1. Check (✓) the places in your home country. Look in your dictionary for help.

Word List: Geography and Habitats		
☐ rain forest	☐ ocean	☐ forest
☐ river	☐ island	☐ lake
☐ desert	☐ beach	☐ mountain range

2. Match to complete the sentences.

_5_ **a.** Miami is the name of a city and a   **1.** desert.

___ **b.** The Pacific is an   **2.** ocean.

___ **c.** Hawaii is a group of   **3.** river.

___ **d.** The Andes is a   **4.** islands.

___ **e.** The Sahara is a   **5.** ~~beach.~~

___ **f.** The Nile is a   **6.** mountain range.

3. Look at the pictures. Circle the correct words.

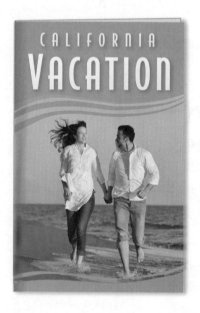

a. Do you like the forest /(ocean)? Come to the California river / beaches.

b. Do you need to relax? How about a quiet ocean / lake in the forest / desert?

c. Are you looking for an exciting place? Come to South America. See the rain forest / desert. Take a trip on the river / mountain range.

1. **Check (✓) the words you know. Look in your dictionary. Find the words you don't know.**

Word List: The Universe

Planets

☐ Mercury   ☐ Jupiter   ☐ moon (new, full)

☐ Venus   ☐ Saturn   ☐ star

☐ Earth   ☐ Uranus   ☐ galaxy

☐ Mars   ☐ Neptune

2. **Cross out the word that doesn't belong.**

   a. Mars   ~~star~~   Earth

   b. Jupiter   full moon   new moon

   c. Saturn   Mercury   galaxy

   d. star   Uranus   moon

   e. planets   stars   universe

3. **Complete the crossword puzzle.**

   ACROSS

   2. Earth, Mars, and Venus are ___.

   5. A full or new ___.

   6. The planet we live on.

   DOWN

   1. A large group of stars.

   3. A cold planet far from the sun.

   4. The sun is a ___.

Trees and Plants

1. Check (✓) the trees and plants in your neighborhood.
Look in your dictionary for help.

Word List: Trees and Plants		
☐ branch	☐ pine	☐ cactus
☐ trunk	☐ palm	☐ vine
☐ root	☐ oak	☐ poison ivy
☐ leaf		

2. Label the trees and plants. Use the words in the box.

| ~~cactus~~ | vine | palm | poison ivy | pine | oak |

a. _____cactus_____

b. _____

c. _____

d. _____

e. _____

f. _____

3. Read the sentences. Write *T* (true) or *F* (false).

a. The leaves grow on the trunk of a tree.   *F*

b. The roots are on the branches.   ____

c. Branches grow from the trunk of a tree.   ____

d. Leaves grow on the branches.   ____

e. All trees have roots.   ____

f. All plants have trunks.   ____

1. Check (✓) the parts of a flower above the soil. Look in your dictionary for help.

> **Word List: Flowers**
>
> ☐ seed   ☐ bud   ☐ sunflower
>
> ☐ roots   ☐ petals   ☐ tulip
>
> ☐ leaves   ☐ stems   ☐ rose

2. Label the flower. Use the words in the box.

> stem   bud   ~~petal~~   leaf   roots   seed

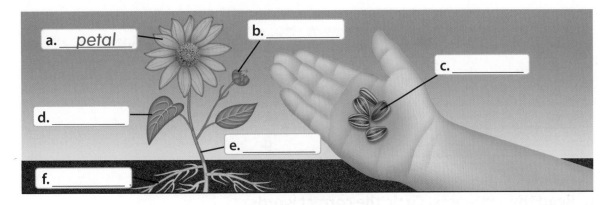

a. ___petal___

b. _____

c. _____

d. _____

e. _____

f. _____

3. Read the article and the sentences. Check (✓) the answers.

a. These flowers are for friends.

  ☐ sunflowers and yellow tulips

  ✓ yellow roses and sunflowers

b. These flowers are for true love.

  ☐ red tulips

  ☐ pink roses

c. These flowers say,
  "You're young and beautiful."

  ☐ white tulips

  ☐ white rosebuds

Say it with Flowers

Do you know that different flowers say different things? For example, one red rose says, **"I love you."** Pink roses say, **"Thank you."** Here are some flowers and what they mean.

GOOD FRIENDS

YOUNG AND BEAUTIFUL

TRUE LOVE

TRUE FRIEND

Marine Life, Amphibians, and Reptiles

1. **Check (✓) the words you know. Look in your dictionary. Find the words you don't know.**

Word List: Marine Life, Amphibians, and Reptiles		
☐ fin	☐ tuna	☐ starfish
☐ gills	☐ octopus	☐ frog
☐ scales	☐ swordfish	
☐ shark	☐ coral	

2. **Write the words in the chart. Use the words in the box.**

| ~~shark~~ | tuna | octopus | swordfish | coral | starfish | frog |

Fins		No Fins	
a.	*shark*	d.	
b.		e.	
c.		f.	
		g.	

3. **Read the sentences. Circle the correct words.**

a. A shark / (frog) can live in the water or out of the water.

b. An octopus / A swordfish has eight arms.

c. A fin / starfish usually has five arms.

d. A gill / swordfish has a long "nose."

e. Some sharks / swordfish can eat fish or people.

f. People buy tuna / scales fresh or in cans.

CHALLENGE Name two things in the Word List with gills.
Name two things in the Word List that don't have scales.

4. Check (✓) the animals that have feet. Look in your dictionary for help.

Word List: Marine Life, Amphibians, and Reptiles			
☐ water	☐ walrus	☐ alligator	☐ lizard
☐ dolphin	☐ sea lion	☐ turtle	☐ snake
☐ whale	☐ rock		

5. Cross out the word that doesn't belong.

a. ~~snake~~   dolphin   whale

b. rock   alligator   lizard

c. walrus   dolphin   turtle

d. sea lion   snake   whale

e. turtle   water   snake

6. Look at the pictures. Answer the questions.

45 feet, 32,000 pounds, 50-60 years

10 feet, 2,700 pounds, 40 years

8 feet, 800 pounds, 14 years

13 feet, 800 pounds, 65 years

2-4 feet, 400 pounds, 50 years

6 feet, 20 pounds, 20 years

a. Which animal is short and heavy?   _____*turtle*_____

b. Which animal lives 50–60 years?   _____

c. Which reptile is 800 pounds?   _____

d. Which animals live 20 years or less?   _____   _____

e. Which animal would you like to be?   _____

Birds, Insects, and Arachnids

1. Check (✓) the animals that have feathers. Look in your dictionary for help.

Word List: Birds, Insects, and Arachnids		
☐ wing	☐ blue jay	☐ butterfly
☐ feather	☐ duck	☐ honeybee
☐ nest	☐ pigeon	☐ spider
☐ owl		

2. Match the words with the pictures.

1.

2.

3.

4.

5.

6.

_3_ **a.** nest   ___ **c.** spider   ___ **e.** pigeon

___ **b.** duck   ___ **d.** butterfly   ___ **f.** feather

3. Read the sentences. Circle the correct words.

a. (Spiders) / Birds don't have wings.

b. Butterflies / Blue jays have feathers.

c. Ducks / Arachnids are birds.

d. Owls / Honeybees are insects.

e. Birds and spiders / butterflies have wings.

f. Spiders are arachnids / birds.

1. Check (✓) the animals in your neighborhood or home.
Look in your dictionary for help.

Word List: Domestic Animals and Rodents			
☐ livestock	☐ horse	☐ rooster	☐ mouse
☐ cow	☐ goat	☐ cat	☐ squirrel
☐ pig	☐ sheep	☐ dog	

2. Unscramble the words.

a. koliecvst   l _i_ _v_ es _t_ oc _k_

b. epesh   s __ __ e __

c. toag   g __ __ t

d. reosh   h __ __ s __

e. sootrer   __ __ __ s t __ r

f. qisurelr   __ q u __ __ __ e __

3. Look at the picture. Circle the correct words.

a. The ⓒat / mouse is sleeping in the sun.

b. The cow / dog is with the sheep.

c. There are three pigs / squirrels.

d. The cow / rooster is eating.

CHALLENGE   Which of the animals in the picture are livestock?

Mammals

1. Check (✓) the words you know. Look in your dictionary. Find the words you don't know.

Word List: Mammals		
☐ coyote	☐ skunk	☐ whiskers
☐ wolf	☐ deer	☐ paw
☐ bear	☐ fox	☐ tail

2. Label the pictures. Use the animals in the Word List.

a. _____ *wolf* _____

b. _____

c. _____

d. _____

e. _____

f. _____

3. Look at the animals in the Word List. Read the sentences. Write *T* (true) or *F* (false).

a. They all are mammals.   _T_

b. They all have tails.   ___

c. They all have paws.   ___

d. They all have whiskers.   ___

e. They all live in the United States.   ___

f. They all live far away from people.   ___

CHALLENGE Do all mammals have tails?

4. Check (✓) the animals you like to see at the zoo. Look in your dictionary for help.

Word List: Mammals			
☐ llama	☐ giraffe	☐ tiger	☐ elephant
☐ monkey	☐ zebra	☐ camel	☐ kangaroo
☐ gorilla	☐ lion		

5. Match the words with the sentences.

_6_ **a.** llama   **1.** It lives in trees.

___ **b.** giraffe   **2.** It lives in Australia.

___ **c.** tiger   **3.** It's black and white.

___ **d.** zebra   **4.** It has a very long neck.

___ **e.** kangaroo   **5.** It's a big cat.

___ **f.** monkey   **6.** ~~It lives in South America.~~

6. Look at the pictures. Check (✓) the correct sentences.

a. ☑ It's a gorilla.

     ☐ It's a llama.

b. ☐ Giraffes have large ears.

     ☐ Elephants walk slowly.

c. ☐ Tigers live alone.

     ☐ Lions live in groups.

d. ☐ Camels live in the desert.

     ☐ Camels have two paws.

Energy and the Environment

1. Check (✓) the words you know. Look in your dictionary. Find the words you don't know.

Word List: Energy and the Environment

☐ solar energy ☐ coal ☐ air pollution

☐ wind power ☐ oil ☐ hazardous waste

☐ natural gas ☐ nuclear energy ☐ water pollution

2. Match the words.

__4__ **a.** solar   **1.** pollution

____ **b.** air   **2.** waste

____ **c.** natural   **3.** gas

____ **d.** wind   **4.** ~~energy~~

____ **e.** hazardous   **5.** power

3. Label the pictures. Use the words in the box.

~~wind power~~ oil coal nuclear energy air pollution water pollution

a. _____wind power_____   b. _____   c. _____

d. _____   e. _____   f. _____

4. Check (✓) the ways you protect the environment. Look in your dictionary for help.

Word List: Energy and the Environment

☐ **reduce** trash   ☐ **turn off** lights   ☐ **plant** a tree

☐ **recycle**   ☐ **carpool**   ☐ the environment

☐ **save** water   ☐ **don't litter**

---

5. Complete the words. Write the letters.

a. r _e_ c y _c_ l e

b. __ a r __ o o __

c. s __ v __ w __ t __ __

d. t __ __ __ e __ vi __ o __ m __ __ t

e. __ __ n' t __ i __ __ e __

f. p __ __ __ t a tr __ __

6. Look at the pictures. Circle the correct words.

a. Ellen (reduces)/ recycles trash.

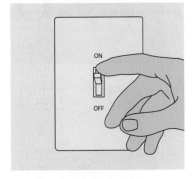

b. Pablo always turns off the litter / lights.

c. Becca and Norma carpool / don't drive to work.

d. Sue saves water / recycles.

e. Glen recycles / plants a tree every year.

f. John and Kate save water / don't litter.

A Graduation

1. **Check (✓) the words you know. Look in your dictionary. Find the words you don't know.**

Word List: A Graduation		
☐ photographer	☐ podium	☐ **take** a picture
☐ funny photo	☐ ceremony	☐ **cry**
☐ serious photo	☐ cap	☐ **celebrate**
☐ guest speaker	☐ gown	

2. **Match the words with the pictures.**

_3_ **a.** guest speaker

___ **b.** gown

___ **c.** podium

___ **d.** photographer

___ **e.** cap

___ **f.** serious photo

___ **g.** funny photo

___ **h.** cry

1.

2.

3.
Thank you.

4.

5.

6.

7.

8.

3. Read the story. Circle the correct words.

a. Here are some photos of my son's graduation (ceremony) / photographer.

b. There's Miguel in his cap and podium / gown.

c. It's a serious / funny photo.

d. This is the guest speaker / photograph.

e. He's in a cap / at the podium.

f. This is Miguel's favorite ceremony / photo.

g. Miguel is crying / celebrating with his friends.

h. It's a funny / serious photo.

4. What about you? Answer the questions. Write *Yes, I do* or *No, I don't.*

a. Do you like to take pictures? _____.

b. Do you like people to take your picture? _____.

c. Do you like to look at photos of other people? _____.

Places to Go

1. Check (✓) the places you like. Look in your dictionary for help.

> ### Word List: Places to Go
>
> ☐ zoo ☐ swap meet ☐ opera
> ☐ movies ☐ aquarium ☐ nightclub
> ☐ botanical garden ☐ play ☐ county fair
> ☐ bowling alley ☐ art museum ☐ classical concert
> ☐ rock concert ☐ amusement park

2. Cross out the word that doesn't belong.

a. ~~nightclub~~   zoo   botanical garden

b. movie   play   swap meet

c. aquarium   nightclub   zoo

d. county fair   classical concert   opera

e. amusement park   art museum   bowling alley

f. rock concert   movie   classical concert

3. Match the words with the pictures.

1. ~~zoo~~   4. swap meet

2. classical concert   5. botanical garden

3. aquarium   6. night club

_1_ a.

___ b.

___ c.

___ d.

___ e.

___ f.

4. Label the picture. Use the words in the box.

| ~~nightclub~~ | bowling alley | movies | opera | rock concert |

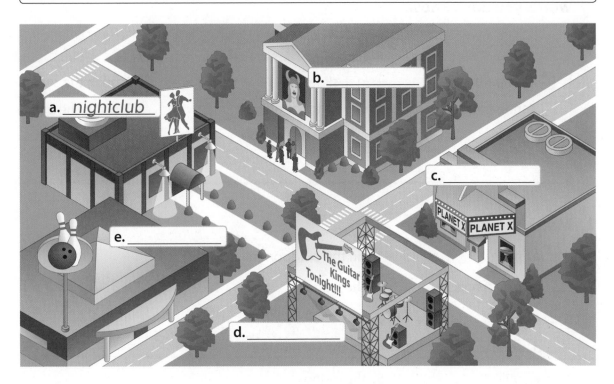

a. _nightclub_

b. _____

c. _____

d. _____

e. _____

5. Read the ads. Answer the questions.

COMMUNITY BULLETIN   PAGE 16

THIS WEEK IN KING CITY

BIG BOB'S BAND – Rock music CITY PARK FRI., 8 P.M. **$5.00**

Mozart's Best – Classical music City Center Sat., 7 p.m. **$12.00**

FUNNY GUY Play MAIN STREET THEATER FRI. – SUN. 8 P.M. **$8.00**

NELSON ART MUSEUM TUES – SUN 8 a.m. – 7 p.m.

King City Aquarium OPEN – 7 DAYS 9 a.m. – 9 p.m.

King County Fair – Now through November Sat., Sun. 8 a.m. – 9 p.m.

a. How many concerts are there?   _____2_____

b. What type of concert is Mozart's Best?   _____

c. What's the name of the play?   _____

d. How much is the rock concert?   _____

e. Is there an amusement park?   _____

f. Where can you see fish and other sea animals?   _____

g. What day is the art museum closed?   _____

229

The Park and Playground

1. **Check (✓) the words you know. Look in your dictionary. Find the words you don't know.**

2. **Match the words.**

_5_ **a.** push   **1.** on the outdoor grill

___ **b.** play tennis   **2.** the wagon

___ **c.** sit   **3.** on the bike path

___ **d.** cook   **4.** on the tennis court

___ **e.** pull   **5.** ~~the swing~~

___ **f.** ride a bike   **6.** on the bench

3. **Label the picture. Use the words in the box.**

~~swings~~   slide   bench   picnic   wagon   bars

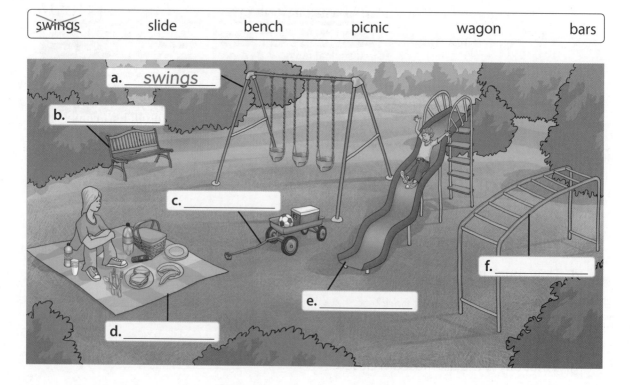

a. _swings_

b. _____

c. _____

d. _____

e. _____

f. _____

1. Check (✓) the things people bring to the beach. Look in your dictionary for help.

Word List: The Beach		
☐ ocean	☐ surfboard	☐ lifeguard
☐ sky	☐ wave	☐ beach chair
☐ sandcastle	☐ pier	☐ sand
☐ beach umbrella		

2. Unscramble the sentences.

a. sky is The blue. _The sky is blue._

b. The large. are waves _____

c. the pier. is The lifeguard on _____

d. a We're making sandcastle. _____

e. the beach. There's sand at _____

3. Look at the picture. Read the sentences. Number the people.

1. Paul has a surfboard.
2. Lou is a lifeguard.
3. Erika is making a sandcastle.
4. Marta is sitting in a beach chair.
5. ~~Ray is in the ocean.~~
6. Grace has a beach umbrella.

1. Check (✓) the things you have. Look in your dictionary for help.

Word List: Outdoor Recreation		
☐ fishing	☐ tent	☐ backpack
☐ camping	☐ sleeping bag	☐ fishing pole
☐ hiking	☐ life vest	☐ canteen

2. Read the sentences. Circle the correct words.

a. Use a tent for (camping) / fishing.

b. Use a life vest for <u>hiking / fishing</u>.

c. Put water in a <u>canteen / sleeping bag</u>.

d. A backpack is good for <u>hiking / fishing</u>.

e. Use a <u>tent / fishing pole</u> for fishing.

f. Camping, fishing, and hiking are types of outdoor <u>recreation / life vests</u>.

3. Read the ad. Answer the questions.

a. How much is the fishing pole? <u>$64.99</u>

b. How much is the backpack? _____

c. How much are the tents? _____

d. Jack buys a fishing pole and a backpack. The tax is $10.04. What is the total? _____

CHALLENGE Look at the ad in Exercise 3. What type of store is this?

1. Check (✓) the sports you like. Look in your dictionary for help.

Word List: Winter and Water Sports			
☐ skiing	☐ ice skating	☐ sailing	☐ snorkeling
☐ snowboarding	☐ waterskiing	☐ surfing	☐ scuba diving

2. Cross out the word that doesn't belong.

a. waterskiing ~~ice skating~~ snorkeling

b. surfing sailing winter sports

c. snowboarding skiing snorkeling

d. snorkeling sailing scuba diving

e. ice skating skiing water sports

3. Look at the pictures. Circle the correct words.

a. He likes waterskiing / (scuba diving.)

b. She likes snorkeling / skiing.

c. She likes winter / water sports.

d. She really likes sailing / surfing.

e. She likes winter / water sports.

f. Her favorite sport is skiing / snowboarding.

1. Check (✓) the things you like to watch. Look in your dictionary for help.

Word List: Individual Sports

- ☐ bowling
- ☐ boxing
- ☐ cycling
- ☐ golf
- ☐ gymnastics
- ☐ skateboarding
- ☐ tennis
- ☐ track and field

2. Match the words with the pictures.

1.
2.
3.
4.
5.

_5_ **a.** boxing

___ **b.** golf

___ **c.** skateboarding

___ **d.** track and field

___ **e.** bowling

3. Label the pictures. Use the words in the box.

| golf | ~~boxing~~ | gymnastics | cycling | tennis | skateboarding |

a. _____boxing_____

b. _____

c. _____

d. _____

e. _____

f. _____

CHALLENGE   Name three individual sports that are dangerous.

1. **Check (✓) the team sports. Look in your dictionary for help.**

Word List: Team Sports	
☐ score	☐ baseball
☐ coach	☐ football
☐ player	☐ soccer
☐ official	☐ ice hockey
☐ basketball	☐ volleyball

2. **Complete the words. Write the letters.**

a. p _l_ a _y_ _e_ r

b. c __ __ c h

c. s __ c c __ __

d. s c __ __ __

e. __ o l l __ __ b __ l l

f. o __ __ i c __ __ l

3. **Study the graph. Answer the questions.**

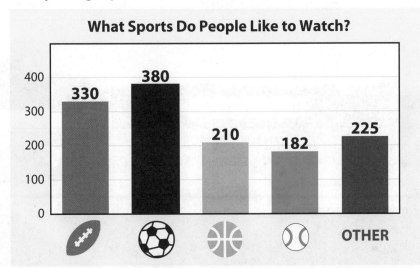

What Sports Do People Like to Watch?

330 380 210 182 225

OTHER

a. What is the favorite sport to watch? _soccer_

b. How many people like to watch basketball? _____

c. How many people like to watch football? _____

d. How many people like baseball? _____

e. Name two "other" team sports. _____

Sports Verbs

1. Check (✓) the things you can do. Look in your dictionary for help.

Word List: Sports Verbs			
☐ pitch	☐ catch	☐ shoot	☐ dive
☐ hit	☐ kick	☐ jump	☐ stretch
☐ throw	☐ pass		

2. Unscramble the words.

a. sasp   p _a_ _s_ s

b. thoso   sh __ __ t

c. ikkc   k __ __ __

d. veid   __ __ v __

e. thicp   p __ __ c __

f. whrot   __ __ r o __

g. pumj   __ __ __ p

h. chertts   __ t __ __ __ c h

3. Label the pictures. Use the words in the box.

throw	~~jump~~	catch	pitch	hit	stretch

a. ___jump___

b. _____

c. _____

d. _____

e. _____

f. _____

CHALLENGE   Look at the picture in Exercise 3. What sport are they playing?

236

1. Check (✓) the things you have at home. Look in your dictionary for help.

Word List: Sports Equipment		
☐ golf club	☐ bowling ball	☐ uniform
☐ tennis racket	☐ soccer ball	☐ baseball
☐ volleyball	☐ baseball bat	☐ football
☐ basketball		

2. Match the words with the pictures.

_5_ **a.** tennis racket

___ **b.** football

___ **c.** baseball

___ **d.** basketball

___ **e.** volleyball

___ **f.** uniform

1.

2.

3.

4.

5.

6.

3. Complete the crossword puzzle.

ACROSS

2. bowling ____

4. ____ equipment

5. tennis ____

DOWN

1. golf ____

2. baseball ____

3. ____ ball

2. B A L L

1. Check (✓) the hobbies you like and the things you have. Look in your dictionary for help.

Word List: Hobbies and Games		
☐ **play** games	☐ dice	☐ oil paint
☐ **paint**	☐ checkers	☐ paintbrush
☐ **knit**	☐ chess	☐ watercolors
☐ **play** cards	☐ glue gun	☐ yarn
☐ video game console	☐ canvas	☐ knitting needles
☐ board game		

2. Write the words in the chart. Use all the words in the Word List.

	Game Words		Hobby Words
a.	*play games*	h.	
b.		i.	
c.		j.	
d.		k.	
e.		l.	
f.		m.	
g.		n.	
		o.	
		p.	

3. Read the sentences. Write *T* (true) or *F* (false).

a. You can paint with watercolors. _T_

b. You need two knitting needles and yarn to knit. ___

c. Chess and cards are board games. ___

d. Checkers is a card game. ___

e. You need two dice for checkers. ___

f. You need a TV or a computer for video games. ___

4. **Look at the picture. Circle the correct words.**

a. Today is Thanksgiving. We're playing <u>hobbies</u> / (<u>games</u>) and having fun.

b. My brothers are playing <u>cards</u> / <u>chess</u>.

c. Our friends are playing a <u>board</u> / <u>paint</u> game.

d. My cousin and I are playing our favorite <u>dice</u> / <u>video</u> game.

e. Grandma is <u>painting</u> / <u>knitting</u>. It's her favorite <u>canvas</u> / <u>hobby</u>.

5. **Study the graph. Answer the questions.**

a. What percent of people like to read? _____ 35% _____

b. What percent like to knit? _____

c. What percent like to paint? _____

d. What is the number one hobby? _____

Electronics and Photography

1. **Check (✓) the things you have at home. Look in your dictionary for help.**

   Word List: Electronics and Photography

   ☐ boom box   ☐ headphones   ☐ DVD player

   ☐ video MP3 player   ☐ flat-screen TV   ☐ speakers

   ☐ dock   ☐ universal remote

2. **Complete the words. Write the letters.**

   a. r _e_ m o _t_ e

   b. d _ _ _ _

   c. D _ D p _ _ y e _

   d. _ _ e a _ e r s

   e. h _ _ d _ h o _ e s

   f. b _ _ _ _ b _ _ _

3. **Label the pictures. Use the words in the box.**

   DVD player   ~~boom box~~   speakers

   video MP3 player   headphones   flat-screen TV

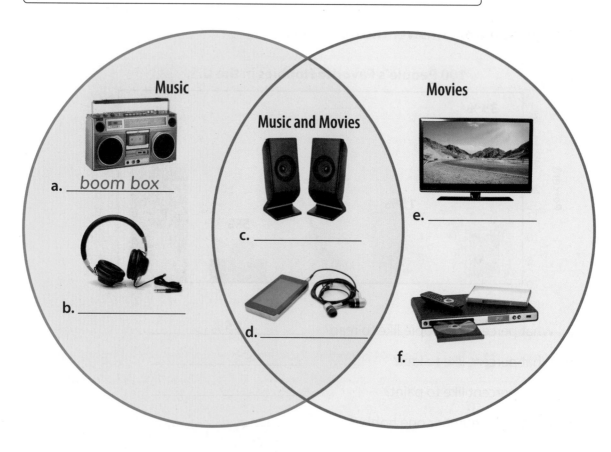

Music

a. _boom box_

b. ___

Music and Movies

c. ___

d. ___

Movies

e. ___

f. ___

240

4. **Check (✓) the words you know. Look in your dictionary. Find the words you don't know.**

Word List: Electronics and Photography		
☐ digital camera	☐ **battery pack**	☐ **rewind**
☐ memory card	☐ **record**	☐ **fast forward**
☐ camcorder	☐ **play**	☐ **pause**

5. **Match the words.**

_2_ **a.** battery   **1.** forward

___ **b.** memory   **2.** ~~pack~~

___ **c.** fast   **3.** card

___ **d.** digital   **4.** the movie

___ **e.** play   **5.** camera

6. **Look at the pictures. Put the sentences in order (1–6).**

___ They record their day at the park.

___ They pause the tape and make popcorn.

_1_ The Ortiz family has a new digital camcorder.

___ Now the children are tired. They fast forward to the end.

___ They play the family movie on their TV.

___ They rewind the funny parts and watch them again.

1. Check (✓) the programs you watch. Look in your dictionary for help.

Word List: Entertainment		
☐ news program	☐ talk show	☐ game show
☐ sitcom	☐ soap opera	☐ sports program
☐ cartoon	☐ reality show	☐ drama

2. Match the words with the sentences.

<u> 5 </u> **a.** news program   **1.** It's for kids.

____ **b.** sitcom   **2.** It's funny.

____ **c.** drama   **3.** It's serious.

____ **d.** sports program   **4.** It shows football, baseball, or other sports.

____ **e.** cartoon   **5.** ~~It tells you about the world.~~

3. Look at the pictures. Write *T* (true) or *F* (false).

a. It's a news program. <u> T </u>

b. It's a reality show. ____

c. It's a soap opera. ____

d. It's a talk show. ____

e. It's a game show. ____

f. It's a sitcom. ____

4. Check (✓) the movies and music you like. Look in your dictionary for help.

Word List: Entertainment		
Types of Movies	**Types of Music**	
☐ comedy	☐ classical	☐ jazz
☐ tragedy	☐ blues	☐ pop
☐ action	☐ rock	
☐ mystery		

5. Cross out the word that doesn't belong.

a. jazz ~~action~~ blues

b. comedy action classical

c. tragedy pop classical

d. rock pop movies

e. music action mystery

6. Label the movie posters. Use the words in the box.

comedy   tragedy   ~~action~~   mystery

a. _action_   b. _____   c. _____   d. _____

Music

1. Check (✓) the words you know. Look in your dictionary. Find the words you don't know.

Word List: Music

☐ **play** an instrument   ☐ clarinet   ☐ trumpet

☐ **sing** a song   ☐ violin   ☐ piano

☐ flute   ☐ guitar   ☐ drums

2. Match the words with the pictures.

1.   2.   3.   4.   5.   6.

_5_ **a.** trumpet   ___ **c.** clarinet   ___ **e.** guitar

___ **b.** flute   ___ **d.** violin   ___ **f.** drums

3. Look at the picture. Read the sentences. Number the people.

1. Jim plays the guitar.

2. Ella sings the songs.

3. ~~Matt plays the drums.~~

4. Scott plays the piano.

5. Miles plays the trumpet.

a. _3_

b. ___

c. ___

d. ___

e. ___

CHALLENGE   Do you play an instrument? What instrument do you play?

1. Check (✓) the words you know. Look in your dictionary. Find the words you don't know.

Word List: Holidays		
☐ parade	☐ mask	☐ feast
☐ fireworks	☐ jack-o'-lantern	☐ ornament
☐ flag	☐ costume	☐ Christmas tree

2. Unscramble the words.

a. readap   p _a_ r a _d_ e

b. fgla   f __ __ __

c. ksam   m __ __ __

d. stafe   f __ __ s __

e. cemtosu   c __ __ t __ __ e

f. kerifsrow   __ __ r e __ o r __ __

3. Label the pictures. Write the numbers.

1. costume
2. ornament
3. fireworks
4. ~~mask~~
5. parade
6. Christmas tree
7. flag
8. jack-o'-lantern

Halloween in the U.S.   a. 4   b. ___

Christmas in Brazil   c. ___   d. ___   e. ___

Chinese New Year in Hong Kong   f. ___   g. ___   h. ___

CHALLENGE   Name a holiday that has fireworks. Name a holiday that has a parade.

A Birthday Party

1. Check (✓) the words you know. Look in your dictionary. Find the words you don't know.

Word List: A Birthday Party		
☐ decorations	☐ **videotape**	☐ **hide**
☐ deck	☐ **make** a wish	☐ **bring**
☐ present	☐ **blow out**	☐ **wrap**

2. Label the pictures. Complete the sentences. Use the words in the box.

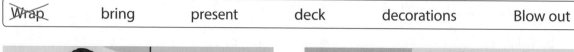

~~Wrap~~   bring   present   deck   decorations   Blow out

a. ____*Wrap*____ the present.

b. The _____ is on the table.

c. The _____ are blue, yellow, and orange.

d. The woman is on the _____.

e. _____ the candles.

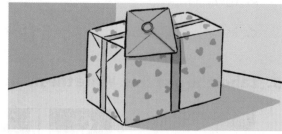

f. We always _____ presents.

246

3. Read the story. Circle the correct words.

a. Today is Ramon's (birthday) / present.

b. There are red and white <u>decks / decorations</u> in the yard.

c. There's a <u>present / wish</u> for Ramon on the deck.

d. Right now Ramon is <u>hiding / making</u> a wish.

e. Then he will <u>wrap / blow out</u> the candles.

f. Ramon's wife is <u>videotaping / making</u> the party.

g. His son is <u>hiding / bringing</u>.

h. Ramon is having a great time at his <u>decorations / party</u>.

4. What about you? Answer the questions. Answer *Yes, I do* or *No, I don't.*

a. Do you like birthday parties? _____.

b. Do you like to give presents to people? _____.

c. Do you like to videotape parties and special events? _____.

247

Look at the picture. There are more than five items that begin with the letter _p_. Find and circle them. Use your dictionary pages 2–29 for help.

Label the pictures. Use the words in the box. Then find the words in the puzzle. Use your dictionary pages 30–45 for help.

| tall | ~~hungry~~ | grandmother | children | exercise |
| bottle | curly | drive | graduate | toddler |

b. _____

c. _____

d. _____

a. _____hungry_____

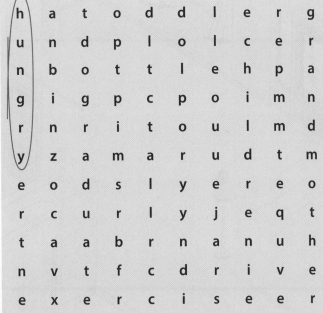

h	a	t	o	d	d	l	e	r	g
u	n	d	p	l	o	l	c	e	r
n	b	o	t	t	l	e	h	p	a
g	i	g	p	c	p	o	i	m	n
r	n	r	i	t	o	u	l	m	d
y	z	a	m	a	r	u	d	t	m
e	o	d	s	l	y	e	r	e	o
r	c	u	r	l	y	j	e	q	t
t	a	a	b	r	n	a	n	u	h
n	v	t	f	c	d	r	i	v	e
e	x	e	r	c	i	s	e	e	r

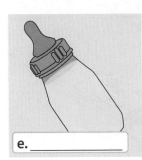

e. _____

f. _____

g. _____

h. _____

i. _____

j. _____

Read the sentences. Complete the picture. Use your dictionary pages 46–65 for help.

a. There's a sofa in the living room.

b. There's a coffee table in front of the sofa.

c. There are a table and two chairs in the kitchen.

d. There's a flowerbed in the yard.

e. There's a dresser in the bedroom.

f. There's a shower in the bathroom.

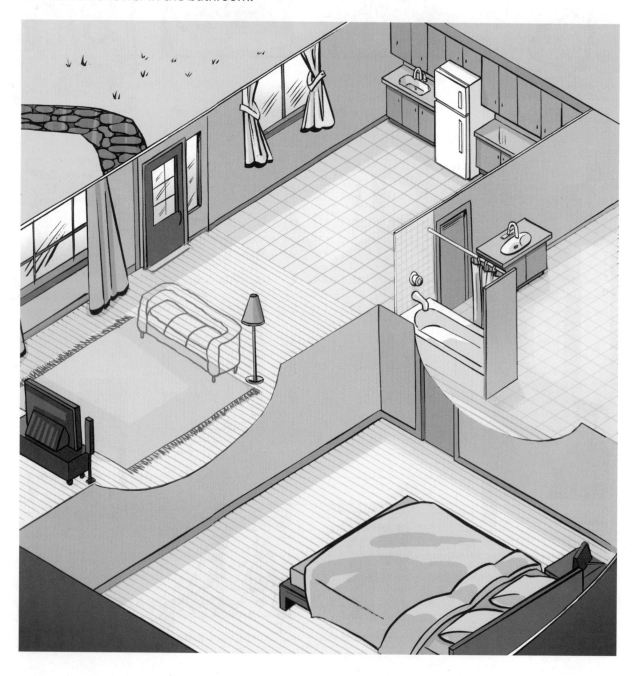

Circle 10 things in the picture from Unit 4. Then write the words below the picture. Use your dictionary pages 66–85 for help.

oranges _____ _____ _____ _____

_____ _____ _____ _____ _____

Read the words. Look at the pictures. Circle the clothes and accessories you see. Use your dictionary pages 86–103 for help.

a.

(blouse)
tie
(briefcase)

b.

sweatpants
T-shirt
shorts

c.

watch
necklace
earrings

d.

evening gown
tuxedo
short skirt

e.

overalls
knit top
sandals

f.

lab coat
robe
pajamas

Label the pictures. Use the words in the box. Then find the words in the puzzle. Use your dictionary pages 104–125 for help.

arm	eye	doctor	headache	heart
mouth	nose	~~nurse~~	toe	toothbrush

a. _nurse_

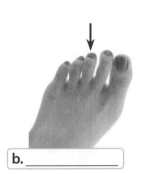

b. _____

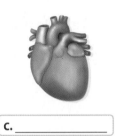

c. _____

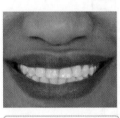

d. _____

t	o	o	t	h	b	r	u	s	h
o	v	n	e	e	y	e	n	h	e
a	m	r	e	a	u	m	d	u	a
f	a	n	u	r	s	e	y	o	d
p	d	o	c	t	o	r	e	l	a
a	r	s	r	r	a	y	r	d	c
r	a	e	s	i	m	o	u	t	h
m	r	m	t	e	i	n	t	o	e

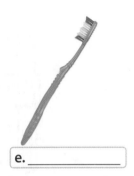

e. _____

f. _____

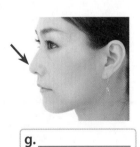

g. _____

h. _____

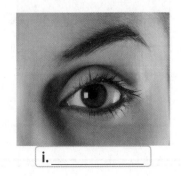

i. _____

j. _____

Another Look (Unit 7)

Read the sentences. Complete the picture. Use your dictionary pages 126–153 for help.

a. There's a coffee shop next to the bookstore.

b. There's a pedestrian in the crosswalk.

c. There's a mailbox next to the bus stop.

d. There's a bus in the street.

e. There's a police officer on the corner.

f. There's litter on the sidewalk.

What's wrong with the picture? Complete the sentences. Use the words in the box. Use your dictionary pages 154–167 for help.

| speed limit | motorcycle | tires | car | ~~bicycle~~ | trunk | taxi | helicopter |

a. The ___bicycle___ is on the building.

e. The _____ is on the sidewalk.

b. The _____ is on the street.

f. The _____ is turning right.

c. The _____ is in the air.

g. The minivan has no _____.

d. The _____ sign says 85.

h. The _____ of the convertible is open.

Label the pictures. Use the words in the box. Then find the words in the puzzle. Use your dictionary pages 168–181 for help.

cashier	training	gardener	repair	~~promotion~~
nurse	resume	interview	application	staff

b. _____

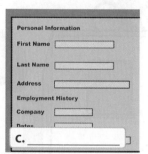

c. _____

d. _____

a. _promotion_

Maria Santos
245 Elm St
Los Angeles
CA 90068

Work Experience:
Smith & Co: Retail Clerk 2 years

e. _____

f. _____

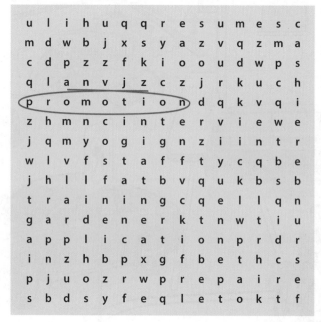

u	l	i	h	u	q	q	r	e	s	u	m	e	s	c
m	d	w	b	j	x	s	y	a	z	v	q	z	m	a
c	d	p	z	z	f	k	i	o	o	u	d	w	p	s
q	l	a	n	v	j	z	c	z	j	r	k	u	c	h
p	r	o	m	o	t	i	o	n	d	q	k	v	q	i
z	h	m	n	c	i	n	t	e	r	v	i	e	w	e
j	q	m	y	o	g	i	g	n	z	i	i	n	t	r
w	l	v	f	s	t	a	f	f	t	y	c	q	b	e
j	h	l	l	f	a	t	b	v	q	u	k	b	s	b
t	r	a	i	n	i	n	g	c	q	e	l	l	q	n
g	a	r	d	e	n	e	r	k	t	n	w	t	i	u
a	p	p	l	i	c	a	t	i	o	n	p	r	d	r
i	n	z	h	b	p	x	g	f	b	e	t	h	c	s
p	j	u	o	z	r	w	p	r	e	p	a	i	r	e
s	b	d	s	y	f	e	q	l	e	t	o	k	t	f

g. _____

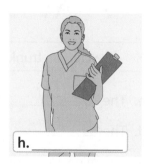

h. _____

i. _____

j. _____

What's wrong with the picture? Complete the sentences. Use the words in the box. Use your dictionary pages 182–199 for help.

| fire extinguisher | hard hat | headset | keyboard | ladder | photocopier |

a. There is water under the computer _____.

b. The _____ _____ is too high on the wall.

c. The _____ is broken.

d. The maintenance worker is not wearing his _____ _____.

e. There's a lot of paper near the _____.

f. The receptionist's _____ is under the desk.

Circle 12 things in the picture from Unit 11. Then write the words below the picture. Use your dictionary pages 200–227 for help.

Today is March 12.

Periodic Table of Elements

planets _____ _____ _____

_____ _____ _____ _____

_____ _____ _____ _____

Circle 10 things in the picture from Unit 12. Then write the words below the picture. Use your dictionary pages 228–247 for help.

paintbrush _____ _____ _____ _____

_____ _____ _____ _____ _____

Verb Guide

Verbs in English are either regular or irregular in the past tense and past participle forms.

Regular Verbs

The regular verbs below are marked 1, 2, 3, or 4 according to four different spelling patterns.
(See page 262 for the irregular verbs, which do not follow any of these patterns.)

Spelling Patterns for the Past and the Past Participle	Example	
1. Add -ed to the end of the verb.	ASK	ASKED
2. Add -d to the end of the verb.	LIVE	LIVED
3. Double the final consonant and add -ed to the end of the verb.	DROP	DROPPED
4. Drop the final y and add -ied to the end of the verb.	CRY	CRIED

The Oxford Picture Dictionary List of Regular Verbs

accept (1)
add (1)
address (1)
adjust (1)
agree (2)
answer (1)
apologize (2)
appear (1)
applaud (1)
apply (4)
arrange (2)
arrest (1)
arrive (2)
ask (1)
assemble (2)
assist (1)
attach (1)
attend (1)
bake (2)
bargain (1)
bathe (2)
block (1)
board (1)
boil (1)
bookmark (1)
borrow (1)
bow (1)
brainstorm (1)
breathe (2)
browse (2)
brush (1)
bubble (2)
buckle (2)
burn (1)
bus (1)
calculate (2)
call (1)

capitalize (2)
carpool (1)
carry (4)
cash (1)
celebrate (2)
change (2)
check (1)
chill (1)
choke (2)
chop (3)
circle (2)
cite (2)
claim (1)
clarify (4)
clean (1)
clear (1)
click (1)
climb (1)
close (2)
collate (2)
collect (1)
color (1)
comb (1)
comfort (1)
commit (3)
compare (2)
complain (1)
complete (2)
compliment (1)
compose (2)
compost (1)
conceal (1)
conduct (1)
consult (1)
contact (1)
convert (1)
convict (1)

cook (1)
cooperate (2)
copy (4)
correct (1)
cough (1)
count (1)
create (2)
cross (1)
cry (4)
dance (2)
debate (2)
decline (2)
delete (2)
deliver (1)
design (1)
dial (1)
dice (2)
dictate (2)
die (2)
direct (1)
disagree (2)
discipline (2)
discuss (1)
disinfect (1)
distribute (2)
dive (2)
divide (2)
double-click (1)
drag (3)
dress (1)
dribble (2)
drill (1)
drop (3)
drown (1)
dry (4)
dust (1)
dye (2)

earn (1)
edit (1)
empty (4)
end (1)
enter (1)
erase (2)
evacuate (2)
examine (2)
exchange (2)
exercise (2)
expire (2)
explain (1)
explore (2)
exterminate (2)
fast forward (1)
fasten (1)
fax (1)
fertilize (2)
fill (1)
finish (1)
fix (1)
floss (1)
fold (1)
follow (1)
garden (1)
gargle (2)
graduate (2)
grate (2)
grease (2)
greet (1)
hail (1)
hammer (1)
hand (1)
harvest (1)
help (1)
hire (2)
hug (3)

identify (4)
immigrate (2)
indent (1)
inquire (2)
insert (1)
inspect (1)
install (1)
introduce (2)
investigate (2)
invite (2)
iron (1)
jaywalk (1)
join (1)
jump (1)
kick (1)
kiss (1)
knit (3)
label (1)
land (1)
laugh (1)
learn (1)
lengthen (1)
lift (1)
list (1)
listen (1)
litter (1)
live (2)
load (1)
lock (1)
log (3)
look (1)
mail (1)
manufacture (2)
match (1)
measure (2)
microwave (2)
milk (1)
misbehave (2)
miss (1)
mix (1)
monitor (1)
mop (3)
move (2)
mow (1)
multiply (4)
negotiate (2)
network (1)
numb (1)
nurse (2)

obey (1)
observe (2)
offer (1)
open (1)
operate (2)
order (1)
organize (2)
overdose (2)
pack (1)
paint (1)
park (1)
participate (2)
pass (1)
paste (2)
pause (2)
peel (1)
perm (1)
pick (1)
pitch (1)
plan (3)
plant (1)
play (1)
polish (1)
pour (1)
praise (2)
preheat (1)
prepare (2)
prescribe (2)
press (1)
pretend (1)
print (1)
program (3)
protect (1)
pull (1)
purchase (2)
push (1)
quilt (1)
race (2)
raise (2)
rake (2)
receive (2)
record (1)
recycle (2)
redecorate (2)
reduce (2)
reenter (1)
refuse (2)
register (1)
relax (1)

remain (1)
remove (2)
renew (1)
repair (1)
replace (2)
report (1)
request (1)
research (1)
respond (1)
retire (2)
return (1)
reuse (2)
revise (2)
rinse (2)
rock (1)
sauté (1)
save (2)
scan (3)
schedule (2)
scroll (1)
scrub (3)
search (1)
seat (1)
select (1)
sentence (2)
separate (2)
serve (2)
share (2)
shave (2)
ship (3)
shop (3)
shorten (1)
shower (1)
sign (1)
simmer (1)
skate (2)
ski (1)
slice (2)
smell (1)
smile (2)
smoke (2)
solve (2)
sort (1)
spell (1)
spoon (1)
staple (2)
start (1)
state (2)
stay (1)

steam (1)
stir (3)
stop (3)
stow (1)
stretch (1)
study (4)
submit (3)
subtract (1)
supervise (2)
swallow (1)
tackle (2)
talk (1)
taste (2)
thank (1)
tie (2)
touch (1)
transcribe (2)
transfer (3)
translate (2)
travel (1)
trim (3)
try (4)
turn (1)
type (2)
underline (2)
undress (1)
unload (1)
unpack (1)
unscramble (2)
update (2)
use (2)
vacuum (1)
videotape (2)
visit (1)
volunteer (1)
vomit (1)
vote (2)
wait (1)
walk (1)
wash (1)
watch (1)
water (1)
wave (2)
weed (1)
weigh (1)
wipe (2)
work (1)
wrap (3)
yell (1)

Verb Guide

Irregular Verbs

These verbs have irregular endings in the past and/or the past participle.

The Oxford Picture Dictionary List of Irregular Verbs

simple	past	past participle	simple	past	past participle
be	was	been	make	made	made
beat	beat	beaten	meet	met	met
become	became	become	pay	paid	paid
bend	bent	bent	picnic	picnicked	picnicked
bleed	bled	bled	proofread	proofread	proofread
blow	blew	blown	put	put	put
break	broke	broken	quit	quit	quit
bring	brought	brought	read	read	read
buy	bought	bought	rewind	rewound	rewound
catch	caught	caught	rewrite	rewrote	rewritten
choose	chose	chosen	ride	rode	ridden
come	came	come	run	ran	run
cut	cut	cut	say	said	said
do	did	done	see	saw	seen
draw	drew	drawn	seek	sought	sought
drink	drank	drunk	sell	sold	sold
drive	drove	driven	send	sent	sent
eat	ate	eaten	set	set	set
fall	fell	fallen	sew	sewed	sewn
feed	fed	fed	shake	shook	shaken
feel	felt	felt	shoot	shot	shot
find	found	found	show	showed	shown
fly	flew	flown	sing	sang	sung
freeze	froze	frozen	sit	sat	sat
get	got	gotten	speak	spoke	spoken
give	gave	given	stand	stood	stood
go	went	gone	steal	stole	stolen
hang	hung	hung	sweep	swept	swept
have	had	had	swim	swam	swum
hear	heard	heard	swing	swung	swung
hide	hid	hidden	take	took	taken
hit	hit	hit	teach	taught	taught
hold	held	held	think	thought	thought
keep	kept	kept	throw	threw	thrown
lay	laid	laid	wake	woke	woken
leave	left	left	win	won	won
lend	lent	lent	withdraw	withdrew	withdrawn
let	let	let	write	wrote	written
lose	lost	lost			